"Lisa Dietlin is all about making a difference. Her latest effort is informative, practical, thought-provoking and a fun read, and provides lots of examples about how easy it can be to get involved with a good cause. Let's all make a difference!"

Bill Horan
Vice President for Development
United States Fund for UNICEF

"Lisa reminds us of the many good people who are dedicated to 'making a difference'. Her commitment to advancing their stories inspires us to take the stage as featured players in making our world better. Her latest book is a wonderful, life-affirming meditation on human service."

Joseph P. Benincasa
President & CEO
The Actors Fund for everyone in entertainment

P9-EJZ-244

Courageous
Dreams
PUBLISHING HOUSE
PO Box 4781 • Chicago, IL • 60680 • 773.772.2402

Book Design by Katie Nordt

Making a Difference III

Still More Tips, Ideas and Stories to Change Your World

Lisa M. Dietlin

Always strive to make a difference!

Dedication

This book is dedicated to all my clients who on
a daily basis change my life by making a difference
in the lives of others!

Acknowledgments

This is my fourth book in four years....just looking at the words on the page make me wonder where the time has gone? There is so much yet to be done to continue making a difference! As with my other books there are so many people to thank!

My first debt of gratitude is to the LMDA staff. They are always on the front lines looking for and sharing experiences, tips, ideas and stories with me. A special thank you to the members of the LMDA Staff including Nadine Donajkowski, Julie Fregetto, Kristen Kepnick, Lorena Alonso, Barbara Figgins, Ashley Pyle, Bianca Andiano, Jessenia Rodriguez, Betty Wazowicz, Anna Fairchild, Lauren Bye, Michael Dietlin, Renee Mula and Kori Edens. As well as our interns this past year including Brittany Wright, Tanisha Dixon, Sarah Dittlinger, Michela Grant and Paige Amdale.

Thanks also to the many, many clients who have inspired us during the past year with their amazing efforts to change the world. It is truly an honor to watch how they try daily to change the world. Many people have asked me over the years where I learned my giving spirit. I believe it begins with one's family. There is a story in my family that when I was about two or three years old, I was hospitalized. My parents had to work so they would visit me during their lunch and other breaks. My mom relates that one day when she arrived there was a net over the crib in which I was placed. This had not been there before and my mom could not understand what had happened. Upon asking one of the nurses on the floor, she was told that during that day I had climbed out of my crib and taken toys from the toy box and slippers from a drawer delivering one of each to the other children on the floor. It seems I thought that if they had slippers and toys they could come out and play. When this story was recently shared with me again it occurred to me that since my youngest days I have had an innate sense to make a difference to give back...maybe I was born this way, who knows? What I do know is that along the way I have had many, many teachers who have set examples to follow including numerous special friends! Thank you to Mary Ann Beckwith, Janet Katowitz, Cathy Cheshire Shook, Caroline Coppola, Marcy Simpson Euler, Kristine Regele Cechovic, Lisa Carr, Paula Regele Ruddock, Heather Glenn, Karen Hynes, Margaret Soffin, Margaret Trimer-Hartley, Tom Ramsden, Charles Katzenmeyer, Julia Koch, Jodie LaRoche, Valerie Ingram, Sandra Mattison, Evelyn Ward, Aimee Daniels, Abby McWilliams, Maria Wynne, Erin Minne', Leticia Herrera, Robert Acton, Renee Torina, Kurt Hill, Sara Davenport, Anne Wisniewski MacArthur, Monica Metzler, Kathryn Tack, Kim Suzor, Jan Pruitt, Lori Kilburg, Mia Hye-ri Baik, Stacy French Reynolds, Suzanne Jurva, Bernie Andary Steiger, Cibeline Sariano and Fr. Zeke Sanchez.

Thanks to my family for their constant support including my mom, Shirley, my sister, Linda, my brother, Jeff and my sister-in-law, Danielle. My nieces and nephews are constant sources of inspiration so a special shout out to Michael, Anna, Benjamin, Nathaniel, Caitlin and Robert. You continue to make a difference! Finally to my godchildren, Annelise Carr, James Noble and Katie Phillips – you all hold a special place in my heart, thanks for just being you...being in my life has made a difference.

As shared in the last book, courage is the virtue I embrace the most in the world. I hope you find courage daily to try to make a difference in your community and world. I am in gratitude to each of you who works everyday to make a difference. You are still on a daily basis inspirational to me and M.A.D. (Making a Difference®) in the world!

Finally, ask yourself this question daily, what are you doing to be M.A.D. (Making A Difference®)?

Lisa M. Dietlin
SUMMER 2012

"*Are you MAD* (Making A Difference®)? Four
(4) Recommended Steps For How To Use This Book"

Step 1: Read a tip every day

Step 2: Try to implement the suggestion or use it as motivation to try to make a difference on a daily basis

Step 3: Write down your reaction to the tip and/or what you did to try to make a difference

Step 4: Submit your stories to MAD@lmdietlin.com [they could be included in the next edition of this book]

Making a Difference ®

I received a "Happy New Year" card from a friend last year. On the front were twelve (12) photos from her trip around the world with her husband. They decided it was now or never and after saving their money they took a year off from life to travel the world. While I know this is something many of us dream of, they did something even more remarkable. They decided to pay attention to the needs of the world. On the card they listed three (3) nonprofit organizations of which they had become aware, encouraging others to learn about them, too. What a wonderful and easy way to make a difference!

_____

_____

_____

_____

_____

_____

_____

_____

_____

_____

_____

_____

_____

_____

_____

Making a Difference®

TIP OF THE DAY

Do you know what the word philanthropy means? It is a noun that means the love and benevolence toward the whole human family; universal good will; desire and readiness to do good for all mankind. Become a philanthropist today and know that by this decision you will be making a difference!

2

TIP OF THE DAY

One in six children and more than 45 million Americans live in poverty. January is Poverty Awareness Month and a most effective way to help is to make a donation to nonprofits helping people in poverty in your community. Consider shelters, soup kitchens, health care clinics, etc. They could use your support—you can make a difference!

Making a Difference®

It has been more than 150 years since the Civil War began in the United States. I learned that Civil War sites are disappearing at the rate of an acre an hour! You can help! To learn more about what happened 150 years ago and the effort to "Preserve Our Past. Protect Our Future", go to give150.com. Your donation will benefit the Civil War Preservation Trust and the National Park Foundation. You can make a difference!

Making a Difference®

John F. Kennedy, the 35th President of the United States said, "Children are the world's most valuable resource and its best hope for the future." How true! Pay attention to the children in your life. Your actions and interactions do make a difference!

_____

_____

_____

_____

_____

_____

_____

_____

_____

_____

_____

_____

_____

_____

_____

_____

_____

_____

_____

_____

_____

_____

_____

_____

Every winter there are those that struggle paying their heating bills. For individuals struggling with heating bills, direct them to LIHEAP which is the federal "Low Income Heating Energy Assistance Program". This program helps those who have a large percentage of their income going to heating. To secure support, contact the state LIHEAP agency to learn how to apply. Share this information with those who can benefit. It will make a difference in someone's life!

Making a Difference®

TIP OF THE DAY

Elie Wiesel, well-known Holocaust victim who survived Auschwitz camp and was awarded the Nobel Peace Prize in 1986 said, "Just as despair can come to one only from other human beings, hope, too, can be given to one only by other human beings." What hope can you give to others that will ultimately make a difference?

_____

_____

_____

_____

_____

_____

_____

_____

_____

_____

_____

_____

_____

_____

_____

_____

_____

_____

_____

TIP OF THE DAY

I attended the opening of the Wounded Warrior Art Exhibit in Chicago. What an amazing show! Sponsored by the Academies of Orthopaedic Surgeons, it is an exhibit of art by medical professionals from their experiences of treating our injured military personnel! Check it out (woundedinactionart.org); see how medical doctors, nurses and others are making a difference in so many ways!

TIP OF THE DAY

The poet Fernanda Miramontes-Landeros said, "Give thanks for what you are now, and keep fighting for what you want to be tomorrow." Think about this statement and determine what you are grateful for today and what you can "fight" for tomorrow that will make a difference!

_____

_____

_____

_____

_____

_____

_____

_____

_____

_____

_____

_____

_____

_____

_____

_____

_____

_____

_____

_____

_____

_____

_____

Making a Difference®

While the source of this quote is unknown, I think it is a relevant statement, "The tragedy of life is not that it ends so soon, but that we wait so long to begin it." Start your day and maybe even begin your life today by committing to help someone else! Take the time to focus on others and see what a difference you will make!

This statement is attributed to Buddha, "Do not dwell in the past, do not dream of the future, concentrate the mind on the present moment." What can you do today, in the present, which will make a difference to others?

_____

_____

_____

_____

_____

_____

_____

_____

_____

_____

_____

_____

_____

_____

_____

_____

_____

_____

_____

_____

_____

Making a Difference®

According to the Environmental Protection Agency (EPA), Americans threw away 250 million tons of trash in 2010. That's 4.4 pounds per person! Think about ways that you can help reduce your own waste, like keeping reusable water bottles, plates and cloth napkins at work to avoid throwing out plastic and paper and buying products with recycled packaging. These are quick and reusable ways to make a difference!

Aeschylus, best known as the father of the Greek tragedy, is quoted as saying, "By polluting clean water with slime you will never find good drinking water." Aeschylus was born in 525 B.C. and lived until 456 B.C. If he knew the value of being attuned to the environment so should we. What can you do today to make a difference in this area?

_____

_____

_____

_____

_____

_____

_____

_____

_____

_____

_____

_____

_____

_____

_____

_____

_____

_____

_____

_____

When I tell people what I do for a living, a number of them tell me about their difficult experiences in trying to help someone or work for a nonprofit organization as a volunteer. I often try to counsel them, but now I think I am going to use this quote by author Shari R. Barr, "Expecting life to treat you well because you are a good person is like expecting an angry bull not to charge because you are a vegetarian." Keep trying to make a difference, even if the bull charges you!

_____

_____

_____

_____

_____

_____

_____

_____

_____

_____

_____

_____

_____

_____

_____

_____

_____

Making a Difference®

Just before 5:00 pm in the evening on January 12, 2010, Haiti was hit by a devastating earthquake. In the blink of an eye, Emily Sanson-Rejouis lost her husband and two of her three children when their 5-story apartment building collapsed. In the face of this tragedy, Emily established the Kenbe La Foundation to honor her fallen family and her husband's goals to give back to the disadvantaged children of Haiti. Kenbe La means 'Never Give Up' in Haitian Creole. The Foundation has been able to open a school in a remote village decimated by the earthquake and give medical aid and temporary shelter to 300+ members of this community. You can learn more and get involved (kenbelafoundation.org). Think of the words "Kenbe La" and how hope and never giving up can apply to helping yourself and others in the world. You will be sure to make a difference.

TIP OF THE DAY

Katherine Anne Porter was a Pulitzer Prize winning journalist who said, "Our being is subject to all the chances of life. There are so many things we are capable of, that we could be or do. The possibilities are so great that we never, any of us, are more than one-fourth fulfilled." Think about what you could do or be that would make a difference!

_____

_____

_____

_____

_____

_____

_____

_____

_____

_____

_____

_____

_____

_____

_____

_____

_____

_____

_____

_____

American novelist, poet and short story writer Charles Bukowski is quoted as saying, "You begin saving the world by saving one man at a time; all else is grandiose romanticism or politics." What a profound statement. Whose world can you change today? It will make a difference!

_____

_____

_____

_____

_____

_____

_____

_____

_____

_____

_____

_____

_____

_____

_____

_____

_____

_____

_____

_____

_____

TIP OF THE DAY

American lyrical poet Sara Teasdale said, "I make the most of all that comes and the least of all that goes." I encourage you to think about this statement today and make the most of all that comes in order to make a difference to others!

Making a Difference®

American football coach and broadcaster Jimmy Johnson said, "The difference between ordinary and extraordinary is that little extra." What "extra" thing could you do today that would make all the difference?

_____

_____

_____

_____

_____

_____

_____

_____

_____

_____

_____

_____

_____

_____

_____

_____

_____

_____

_____

_____

_____

_____

Annually, Al Roker, the national weatherman with NBC's morning news program *Today* travels the country with the "Lend a Hand" Tour. Since 2002, Al Roker has helped smaller nonprofits throughout the country improve their communities by surprising them with truckloads of items. The idea came after 9/11 when many donations were redirected. It is an effort to shine a light on those lesser known nonprofit organizations that are daily making a difference!

_____

_____

_____

_____

_____

_____

_____

_____

_____

_____

_____

_____

_____

_____

_____

_____

_____

Making a Difference®

The well-known physicist Albert Einstein, who won the Nobel Prize for Physics in 1921, said, "Only one who devotes himself to a cause with his whole strength and soul can be a true master. For this reason, mastery demands all of a person." How very true! What can you work to master in your community that would make a difference?

_____

_____

_____

_____

_____

_____

_____

_____

_____

_____

_____

_____

_____

_____

_____

_____

_____

_____

_____

_____

TIP OF THE DAY

Thomas Edison, probably the most famous American inventor holding over 1000 patents, said, "Genius is 1% inspiration and 99% perspiration." It is great advice for us to heed in the nonprofit world. In other words, what idea do you have that if you worked hard to make it reality would make a difference?

_____

_____

_____

_____

_____

_____

_____

_____

_____

_____

_____

_____

_____

_____

_____

_____

_____

_____

_____

_____

Making a Difference®

I love this quote by motivational speaker Anthony Robbins. He said, "Live life fully while you're here. Experience everything. Take care of yourself and your friends. Have fun, be crazy, be weird. Go out and screw up! You're going to anyway, so you might as well enjoy the process. Take the opportunity to learn from your mistakes: find the cause of your problem and eliminate it. Don't try to be perfect; just be an excellent example of being human." Consider this statement today and see if you can live your life in way that will take this into consideration with the end result being you making a difference!

Ever heard of Fossil Rim Wildlife Center? It is a nonprofit organization that specializes in captive breeding programs for indigenous and exotic animals that are endangered or threatened. Founded by a Fort Worth, Texas businessman named Tom Mantzel who was concerned and passionate about the loss of wild habitat and species that were becoming extinct, the Fossil Rim Wildlife Center is the first facility to be accredited by the American Zoo and Aquarium Association. Check it out (fossilrim.org) and learn what one man did to make a difference!

_____

_____

_____

_____

_____

_____

_____

_____

_____

_____

_____

_____

_____

_____

_____

Making a Difference®

TIP OF THE DAY

While the author of this quote is unknown the statement is powerful, "Many of the great accomplishments of the world were accomplished by tired and discouraged men who kept on working." Keep working; don't get discouraged. By this simple act you will be making a difference!

_____

_____

_____

_____

_____

_____

_____

_____

_____

_____

_____

_____

_____

_____

_____

_____

_____

_____

_____

_____

Making a Difference®

The Global Soap Project (globalsoap.org)

is a nonprofit organization dedicated to saving lives. It takes discarded soap from hotels and reprocesses it into new bars of soap. These are then given and distributed to vulnerable populations throughout the world. Located in Atlanta, Georgia, it was founded by a former Ugandan who escaped with his family named Derrick Kayongo. He had experienced first-hand what happens to people living displaced in refugee camps. The Global Soap Project also works to raise the understanding of what a lack of sanitation does to people. There are more than 4.6 million hotel rooms in the United States and it is estimated that daily over 2.6 million bars of soap are discarded. We can do better. Check out this unique nonprofit organization and see how you can help to make a difference!

TIP OF THE DAY

Pierre Corneille, a French playwright and poet who lived in the 17th century, said, "The manner of giving is worth more than the gift." Think about this statement. What gift or donation could you make today? How will you give it? If you follow Pierre's advice, the manner in which you give makes all the difference!

_____

_____

_____

_____

_____

_____

_____

_____

_____

_____

_____

_____

_____

_____

_____

_____

_____

_____

The Philadelphia Orchard Project has a group of volunteers plant trees in city orchards. To date more than 200 fruit trees have been planted in 23 city orchards. By their actions, these folks are working daily to make a difference!

Did you know you can get audiobooks for free? Go to LibriVox.org which is a worldwide digital library with more than 4000 unabridged classic books available. Books by Charles Dickens, Louisa May Alcott, Henry Adams and others are available as well as plays and poetry. You can also volunteer to be a reader! Check this site out as well as literalsystems.org and audiobooksforfree.com. You could learn the great classics or become a volunteer reader...both options will make a difference!

_____

_____

_____

_____

_____

_____

_____

_____

_____

_____

_____

_____

_____

_____

_____

Have you heard of Craig Roberts and Fiamma di Gioria? They are a couple ages 61 and 72 respectively that decided to adopt children when they were in their "retirement" years. Craig and Fiamma, who live in Minnesota, adopted two teenagers and their 10 year old sibling. They say, "It's a way to give back, to have an impact each and every day." Thanks to Craig and Fiamma as well as the others who are changing their lives and making difference!

Making a Difference®

Salem Harvest was founded in January 2010 by a group of neighbors who wanted to be sure food banks had fresh product from private sources. In their first season which ran from July to November, the organization had 1700 volunteers who picked 53,000 pounds of vegetables and fruits on local farms and then delivered the produce to various food programs. An additional benefit was that the program allowed volunteers to keep half of what they harvested. What a great idea and a relatively easy way for many to make a difference!

Making a Difference®

$\mathcal{S}$tarted in 1926, February has been designated as Black History Month. The purpose is the remembrance of important people and events in African American history. Take time this month to learn more about a history many of us never studied in school, attend functions, watch news programs and read to learn more. By becoming aware of others' histories, we learn more about ourselves and can make a difference.

Making a Difference®

In 2011, Toyota announced a plan to salute do-gooders by donating 100 cars over 100 days to nonprofit organizations that could use a new vehicle. They did this via a number of ways including Facebook and teaming up with the *Today* show's "Lend a Hand" program. The program continues today. Thanks to Toyota for making a difference in such a unique way!

Making a Difference®

Albert J. Madden, known as Buddy, is 92 years old and still shows up to play taps at military funerals. He estimates he has played this tune at more than 3500 funerals, memorials and ceremonies; he says he still gets emotional every single time. Buddy was in the military for 27 years and played (sometimes leading) more than 19 bands. In 2010 he earned the distinction of being the oldest bugler to play at Arlington National Cemetery. Thank you Buddy Madden for making a difference!

_____

_____

_____

_____

_____

_____

_____

_____

_____

_____

_____

_____

_____

_____

_____

_____

_____

The American novel author Tom Robbins is credited with saying, "Stay committed to your decisions, but stay flexible in your approach." What do you want to change in your community? Is there another approach you could take to accomplish your goals? What other ways are there to achieve your goal of making a difference?

_____

_____

_____

_____

_____

_____

_____

_____

_____

_____

_____

_____

_____

_____

_____

_____

_____

_____

_____

_____

_____

Making a Difference®

What do Brett Michaels, Halle Berry, Jay Cutler, Mary Tyler Moore, Nick Jonas, Patti LaBelle and Paul Sorvino have in common? All have been diagnosed with diabetes and are living successful lives with it. More than 25 million people have diabetes in the United States and don't know it. Get tested; by doing this you will be making a difference!

Making a Difference®

I purchased a bottle of Flip Flop wine. On the wine bottle there was a tag that said, "Together We Can Help". For every bottle of wine purchased, one pair of flip flops will be donated to the nonprofit organization Soles 4 Souls. What a clever marketing idea. Check out the nonprofit (soles4-souls.org) which began after the Tsunami in 2004 with the simple concept of procuring shoes and getting them to those in need. Every seven (7) seconds another pair of shoes is distributed. This nonprofit is definitely making a difference.

Looking for new donors to a nonprofit organization you run or for which you are supposed to raise money? Have you considered working with the entrepreneurs in your community? Even in tough economic times, there are entrepreneurs running successful businesses and making money. Check out how to approach them by reading my first book, *Transformational Philanthropy: Entrepreneurs and Nonprofits*. By reading this book and working with entrepreneurs, you will be making a difference!

_____

_____

_____

_____

_____

_____

_____

_____

_____

_____

_____

_____

_____

_____

_____

_____

_____

_____

TIP OF THE DAY

Lord Chesterfield was a British Diplomat and statesman born in 1694 who said, "Know the true value of time; snatch, seize, and enjoy every moment of it. No idleness, no delay, no procrastination; never put off till tomorrow what you can do today." Follow this advice. What can you do today (and not put off) that will make a difference in your community and to others?

_____

_____

_____

_____

_____

_____

_____

_____

_____

_____

_____

_____

_____

_____

_____

_____

_____

_____

_____

Making a Difference®

A very popular television show on cable is *Army Wives*. It is the story of five (5) women and their lives. What is most amazing about this television series is how often they promote a nonprofit organization within the storyline or list a cause they are supporting on the show's website. More and more television programs are incorporating a charitable theme. This season notice how your favorite TV program might feature a cause or highlight an issue. This incorporation truly makes a difference!

Making a Difference®

It seems as if every weekend you can participate in an "-athon" type fundraiser for a nonprofit organization. Many of these endurance events are fundraisers to benefit health related organizations such as the Susan G. Komen Race for the Cure (breast cancer) or Easter Seals' Walk with Me for Autism. Such contests raise both funds and awareness about their respective disease or illness. The idea of people raising money for charity by walking, running or bicycling began in 1970 when the March of Dimes organized and launched its first WalkAmerica event. It was such a success that the idea was copied, adopted and adapted by many nonprofit organizations. This year consider walking, running or biking to make a difference for your favorite charitable cause.

The great writer Ralph Waldo Emerson said, "You cannot do a kindness too soon because you never know how soon it will be too late." Words to live by every day and to insure that you will be make a difference!

_____

_____

_____

_____

_____

_____

_____

_____

_____

_____

_____

_____

_____

_____

_____

_____

_____

_____

_____

_____

_____

_____

The famed artist Vincent van Gogh said, "The fishermen know that the sea is dangerous and the storm is terrible, but they have never found these dangers sufficient reason for remaining ashore." What changes do you see that need to be made in your community which appear dangerous? What could you do to change this paradigm and make a difference?

_____

_____

_____

_____

_____

_____

_____

_____

_____

_____

_____

_____

_____

_____

_____

_____

_____

_____

Making a Difference®

We often don't think of our fathers when we think of charitable activities, it is usually our mothers that most of us remember putting together food baskets or helping a neighbor. But let's pay attention to the role our dads play in the nonprofit world. Think of where the Boy Scouts would be without our dads serving as den fathers and leaders. They are often the ones in the middle of the wilderness or forests teaching their sons how to camp, start a fire, fish, etc. Consider how many dads serve as coaches for t-ball, little league, basketball, hockey and soccer teams. They often give up hours of their time to help their sons and other boys as well as their daughters in the community become better athletes. Take time to thank your dad for making a difference in the charitable world!

_____

_____

_____

_____

_____

_____

_____

_____

_____

_____

_____

_____

Making a Difference®

You may recognize Green Bay Packer Donald Driver for his fancy footwork on *Dancing with the Stars* and the football field. You may not know that growing up, Driver, his mother and his three siblings were often homeless. Sports were his way out of a life of hardship. He now aids the homeless and promotes the importance of education and good health through The Donald Driver Foundation (donaldriverfoundation.com). Donald Driver is a true triple threat: a winner on the dance floor, the football field and in the eyes of those helped by his foundation. Thank you, Donald Driver, for making a difference!

TIP OF THE DAY

Most of us have heard of the Better Business Bureau but did you know they have a charitable giving division? The Better Business Bureau's Wise Giving Alliance monitors, reviews and gives their charity seal of approval to national nonprofit organizations that meet their 20 standards. Check them out (bbb.org/us/charity) and see how you can use this service to make a difference!

_____

_____

_____

_____

_____

_____

_____

_____

_____

_____

_____

_____

_____

_____

_____

_____

_____

_____

_____

_____

Making a Difference®

Did you know that surveys show people who work in the nonprofit sector are happier and healthier? Have you ever considered a career in the nonprofit sector? More than 12 million people or 9% of the US workforce is employed by a nonprofit organization. Check it out and consider doing good as your career. By simply going to work and doing your job you can make a difference!

Today there are many educational and training programs for individuals wishing to enter the nonprofit field. A simple search on the Internet can identify them and you can begin to investigate which ones fit your needs and lifestyle. By becoming more knowledgeable about the nonprofit field, you will be making a difference!

_____

_____

_____

_____

_____

_____

_____

_____

_____

_____

_____

_____

_____

_____

_____

_____

_____

_____

Making a Difference®

TIP OF THE DAY

While the author is unknown, this is a relevant statement to consider, "Never miss an opportunity to make others happy, even if you have to leave them alone in order to do it." By trying to follow this advice, you will be making a difference!

49

Making a Difference®

I recently learned about Carlo Lorenzo Garcia, an actor whom my friend Barbara knows. She told me that for a year he was going to do something for others. His website says, "An ordinary guy's guide to giving back every day. My name is Carlo and my mission is to give to charity every day for a year. This mission is built on a belief that you don't have to be rich in dollars to make a difference, you only need to be rich in spirit. I may not always be able to give a lot, but I will Give Every day. I'm just a regular joe. I grew up on the south side of Chicago. I don't come from money. I don't have a lot of money. Growing up, my family would scrape by, yet somehow us kids were always fed and clothed with a roof over our heads. So, I dedicate this journey to my mom for showing me that you can do so much even when you have very little." Thanks Carlo for leading by example and making a difference!

Making a Difference®

Support the arts in your community! Often during economic downturns, financial support to arts and cultural institutions can decline taking a back seat to the immediate needs of many in the community. Consider making a donation annually to an arts or cultural organization to insure your favorite museum, gallery, sculpture garden, etc. is open. One way to do this is to become a member. By visiting the institution, making a donation or as suggested becoming a member you will be making a difference!

TIP OF THE DAY

Have you heard of GoHYHO, which stands for Go Help Yourself Help Others (GoHYHO.com)? It is a new initiative to connect great consumer deals with charitable giving opportunities. GoHYHO is a new way to fund and follow nonprofit organizations in their local communities. GoHYHO will feature local business deals, building in an opportunity for shoppers to donate to nonprofits. Check them out and see a new and innovative way to make a difference!

_____

_____

_____

_____

_____

_____

_____

_____

_____

_____

_____

_____

_____

_____

_____

_____

_____

TIP OF THE DAY

Marian Wright Edelman is an American activist for the rights of children. She said, "Education is for improving the lives of others and for leaving your community and world better than you found it." Educate yourself about an issue in your community then work to change or improve the situation. You will be making a difference!

_____

_____

_____

_____

_____

_____

_____

_____

_____

_____

_____

_____

_____

_____

_____

_____

_____

_____

_____

_____

_____

_____

Have you ever heard of the Ravinia Festival? Located just north of Chicago, it started in 1904 and is the oldest summer music festival in the US and also a nonprofit organization. You can sit in the amphitheater or on the lawn, bring a picnic, meet friends and listen to great music performed live! Check it out (ravinia.org) and learn about how many in the Chicago area enjoy summer and music. The Ravinia Festival makes a difference.

Have you heard of Born Learning? It is a public service campaign to help parents, grandparents, caregivers and others realize and turn everyday situations in learning moments for children. Many are concerned that our children are entering school unprepared but parents and others often feel they don't have the time to "teach". Check out this innovative campaign (bornlearning.org) that was started by the United Way of America, the Ad Council, Civitas and Families and Work Institute. By paying attention you can turn everyday acts into learning moments and you will be making a difference!

Author, writer and American mythologist Joseph Campbell said, "The big question is whether you are going to be able to say a hearty yes to your adventure." What adventure could you say yes to that would help others in your community? Sometimes simply saying yes to some new adventure, strategy or plan will make the difference!

Making a Difference®

Have you heard of the Jaipur Limb? It was created in the 1960s by an orthopedic surgeon and an artisan sculptor with a fourth grade education in response to the hospital not offering limbs to poor people who could not afford them. They did not patent their design and anyone can use it. Today the materials for each limb are estimated to cost approximately $35-45 with the total cost of the leg with labor, etc. estimated to be at $100 – 200. The limb is designed for the specific needs of its most frequent uses and is durable, often lasting three years. Thanks to Pramad Karan Sethi and Ram Chadra for truly making a difference!

When Prince William married Catherine (Kate) Middleton in the spring of 2011, they asked that in lieu of gifts donations be made to charity. Within two months of their nuptials, more than $1.6 million had been donated and would be dispersed to their pre-determined favorite charities. William and Kate used their special day to direct funds to charities in Great Britain, Australia, Canada and New Zealand! Thanks to them for making a difference!

_____

_____

_____

_____

_____

_____

_____

_____

_____

_____

_____

_____

_____

_____

_____

_____

_____

_____

Making a Difference®

Just say the word "Walmart" and look for the wide variety of responses you will get from people. There are those individuals that hate this corporate giant and those that love it. What I choose to focus on is their philanthropic and charitable work. In 2010, Walmart pledged $2 billion in food and aid over the next five (5) years to feed hungry people. The donation will go to Feeding America (feedingamerica. org), which leads the nation's network of more than 200 food banks. It is estimated that annually, Americans throw out $150 billion worth of food, primarily due to cosmetic imperfections or lack of understanding about expiration dates. Through Walmart's generosity people will be fed! Now that's making a difference!

_____

_____

_____

_____

_____

_____

_____

_____

_____

_____

_____

_____

_____

Albert Szent-Gyorgyi, the biochemist and winner of the Nobel Prize, said, "Discovery consists of seeing what everybody has seen and thinking what nobody has thought." This is especially true in the nonprofit sector. What does everybody see, but you think differently about? Could these thoughts affect change and make a difference?

_____

_____

_____

_____

_____

_____

_____

_____

_____

_____

_____

_____

_____

_____

_____

_____

_____

_____

_____

Making a Difference®

I love this quote by the author Les Brown, "Life takes on meaning when you become motivated, set goals and charge after them in an unstoppable manner." Follow this advice and you will be making a difference!

_____

_____

_____

_____

_____

_____

_____

_____

_____

_____

_____

_____

_____

_____

_____

_____

_____

_____

_____

_____

Making a Difference®

In 2011, at the age of 104, Huguette Clark died. She was heir to the fortune from a Montana copper mine and reportedly worth $400 million. Even though she was a recluse living in almost total isolation for the last 20 years of her life, she still cared about people. She left the majority of her fortune to charity including the wishes that her California estate become a museum to house her art collection as well as her rare books and musical instruments. Huguette Clark might have been a recluse in life but upon her death she became a very public philanthropist. She made a difference!

Making a Difference®

Heifer International (heifer.org) offers you the opportunity to donate animal gifts in someone's name to families in need. Think of the fun you can have purchasing a cow, flock of geese or water buffalo and letting the recipient know what their gift is doing to help others. Considering giving gifts via Heifer International during the next year! By doing this you will be making a difference in so many ways!

Making a Difference®

American novelist and playwright James Baldwin said, "No one can possibly know what is about to happen; it is happening each time, for the first time, for the only time." You don't know what change your actions could precipitate or cause. Work to make a difference!

_____

_____

_____

_____

_____

_____

_____

_____

_____

_____

_____

_____

_____

_____

_____

_____

_____

_____

_____

_____

_____

_____

TIP OF THE DAY

Tom Krause, a motivational speaker, coach and teacher, is credited with saying, "If you only do what you know you can do – you never do very much." This statement is very true! Push yourself beyond what you know you can do. You will be amazed at how with little effort you can make a huge difference!

_____

_____

_____

_____

_____

_____

_____

_____

_____

_____

_____

_____

_____

_____

_____

_____

_____

_____

_____

Making a Difference®

The Foundation for Sarcoidosis Research (FSR) is doing amazing work. Founded in 2000 by Andrea and Reading Wilson, it works to fund research for this terrible devastating disease. Sarcoidosis is an inflammatory disease that can affect almost any organ in the body and is often misdiagnosed for years. Check it out (stopsarcoidosis. org) and see how a dedicated group of individuals, including actress Tea' Leoni, model and MTV VJ Karen "Duffy" Duff-Lambros and former Boston Celtic/NBA Champion Bill Russell, is tackling this difficult disease. They are truly making a difference!

Former First Lady Eleanor Roosevelt said, "A women is like a tea bag. You never know how strong she is until she gets into hot water." Think about the women in your life and how strong they are when the get involved with a cause for which they care and have passion. These women often dismiss the naysayers and focus on making a difference!

Making a Difference®

Riding the Chicago "L" I read this ad, "Colon cancer kills as many women as ovarian, cervical and uterine cancers combined." This statement took my breath away! Then I began thinking about what I could do to change this situation. I realized I could make a financial donation for research or patient support; I could become aware and share this information with other women (and men) encouraging them to be tested regularly. I could make sure I take care of my health and get tested. All of these seemingly simple things could and do make a difference!

_____

_____

_____

_____

_____

_____

_____

_____

_____

_____

_____

_____

_____

_____

_____

Thomas Jefferson, the third President of the United States and author of the Declaration of Independence, said, "It is more honorable to repair a wrong than to persist in it." What powerful advice to follow. What wrong do you see in your community that you could fix? You can be assured your efforts will make a difference!

Making a Difference®

Dr. Joe Vitale has as part of his email signature block the following phrase: "Aude aliquid dignum" which tells the reader this is 16th century Latin for "Do Something Worthy". A great mantra to live by; a guaranteed way to make a difference!

_____

_____

_____

_____

_____

_____

_____

_____

_____

_____

_____

_____

_____

_____

_____

_____

_____

_____

_____

_____

_____

_____

TIP OF THE DAY

$\mathcal{H}arry$ $\mathcal{S}.$ $\mathcal{T}ruman$ was the 33rd President of the United States. He said, "Men make history, and not the other way around. In periods where there is no leadership, society stands still. Progress occurs when courageous skillful leaders seize the opportunity to change things for the better." Seize the opportunity to change things today! Your efforts will make a difference!

_____

_____

_____

_____

_____

_____

_____

_____

_____

_____

_____

_____

_____

_____

_____

_____

_____

_____

_____

_____

The famed film director Alfred Hitchcock said, "There is no terror in a bang, only in the anticipation of it." Don't be afraid of the bang that will occur when something changes, simply work to make a difference!

_____

_____

_____

_____

_____

_____

_____

_____

_____

_____

_____

_____

_____

_____

_____

_____

_____

_____

_____

_____

_____

He has played the television characters of Peter Florick, Mike Logan and Mr. Big, but Chris Noth is using his high profile to raise awareness about diabetes. It is estimated that more than 25 million have diabetes and 7 million do not know they have the disease. There is a national campaign to create awareness with the message "Ask. Screen. Know." to promote screening and education. Chris Noth joins other high profile personalities such as Paul Sorvino and his daughter, Mira, in raising awareness. Together they are making a difference!

_____

_____

_____

_____

_____

_____

_____

_____

_____

_____

_____

_____

_____

_____

_____

_____

Making a Difference®

There is no statue dedicated to him in his hometown of Freehold, New Jersey; as a matter of fact the city has voted down several proposals that would erect a statue as well as naming a street after him. But regardless of the lack of public recognition, singer, songwriter and rocker Bruce Springsteen is a very charitable person and committed to giving back. Rumor has it that no matter what town he plays in, he makes a charitable donation, usually to a local food bank or pantry. Bruce Springsteen is definitely making a difference in both the music and philanthropic worlds!

TIP OF THE DAY

Expect the best from people! You will be amazed at what they can do and how this simple but profound expectation will make a difference!

_____
_____
_____
_____
_____
_____
_____
_____
_____
_____
_____
_____
_____
_____
_____
_____
_____
_____
_____
_____
_____
_____
_____
_____

Many of us dread attending conferences or meetings thinking what are we going to learn? Why not change your attitude and think about what you could learn? I always try to focus on the positive saying if I can learn one new thing or meet one new person, then the conference or meeting was worthwhile. Change your attitude and you will be amazed how it makes a difference!

Making a Difference®

Singer and songwriter Sheryl Crow is most well known for her musical talents. However, if you visit her website (sherylcrow.org) you will see her commitment to charitable endeavors. Sheryl Crow provides links to more than ten (10) nonprofit organizations and causes from breast cancer (of which she is a survivor) to saving wild horses! Check it out and see how Sheryl Crow is making a difference...and how you can, too!

_____

_____

_____

_____

_____

_____

_____

_____

_____

_____

_____

_____

_____

_____

_____

_____

_____

_____

TIP OF THE DAY

Inventor and psychologist J.J. Gordon said, "If we are to perceive all the implications of the new, we must risk, at least temporarily, ambiguity and disorder." This statement is true especially as we try new things to change the world. Our willingness to endure ambiguity and disorder just might be what makes the difference.

_____

_____

_____

_____

_____

_____

_____

_____

_____

_____

_____

_____

_____

_____

_____

_____

_____

_____

_____

_____

TIP OF THE DAY

They say more than 66% of us volunteer annually! Do your part; find a way to volunteer. It does make a difference!

_____

_____

_____

_____

_____

_____

_____

_____

_____

_____

_____

_____

_____

_____

_____

_____

_____

_____

_____

_____

_____

_____

Making a Difference®

$\mathcal{O}ne\ of\ my\ favorite$ childhood memories is picking blueberries with family members, especially my siblings, when we lived in Montrose, Michigan. Doing things together is often the glue that keeps a family intact. Consider what you could do at your age with your family members. Trust me, it will not only create childhood memories but also make a difference!

Making a Difference®

I was having dinner with my friend Father Zeke and he shared he had learned from me that everyone has something to contribute. They often just need to be asked. I told him that I still agreed with that statement and had recently learned from another friend that even contributing a smile can and often does make a difference! So smile today at all you meet and see how you are making a difference!

Making a Difference®

I often hear people make statements about giving up on something before they even get started, especially if a problem seems insurmountable. It is as if they are unwilling to challenge themselves to do good. I recommend a change of attitude. Challenge yourself daily to do good and give back to your community and others. By simply changing your attitude, you will be making a difference!

Making a Difference®

TIP OF THE DAY

Most of us are familiar with the book *Life's Little Instruction Book* with its quick wit and advice. One of my favorites is, "You must take action now that will move you towards your goals. Develop a sense of urgency in your life." Good advice to follow. Be urgent with the actions to change your community. It will make a difference!

TIP OF THE DAY

The famed film producer and director Billy Wilder said, "Trust your own instinct. Your mistakes might as well be your own, instead of someone else's." Think about this statement and then about what your instinct is telling you to do. Try it...it just might make a difference!

Making a Difference®

Many of us are looking for bargains these days! The Michigan Design Center has an Annual Sample Sale. In 2011, they donated a portion of the admission price of $5 to the WDET 101.9 FM Detroit Public Radio. Simply attending this event and paying the admission price made a difference. What could you participate in within your community that would make a difference?

_____

_____

_____

_____

_____

_____

_____

_____

_____

_____

_____

_____

_____

_____

_____

_____

_____

_____

Making a Difference®

Jonathan Swift, who lived in the 17th century and was an Anglo-Irish satirist, essayist and political pamphleteer as well as a poet, said, "Vision is the art of seeing things invisible." What do you see in your community that appears invisible to others? Speak up about it. Take action. You will be making a difference!

_____

_____

_____

_____

_____

_____

_____

_____

_____

_____

_____

_____

_____

_____

_____

_____

_____

_____

_____

_____

Making a Difference®

One day last year my neighbor Lauren sent this message, "We have an enormous basil plant on our front stoop. Please help yourself!!! Honestly there is no way I would be able to use it all — help a neighbor out and save a few bucks. Just bring your own scissors and snip away any time!" This simple little message and act made a difference! Follow Lauren's example and consider what you could offer to your neighbors that would make a difference?

_____

_____

_____

_____

_____

_____

_____

_____

_____

_____

_____

_____

_____

_____

_____

_____

_____

_____

A Japanese Proverb says, "Fall seven times, stand up eight." I love this statement. Don't give up when undertaking things that will change your community. Keep trying; keep getting up; keep working to make a difference!

Making a Difference®

The Indian Spiritual leader Swami Vivekananda said, "Take up one idea. Make that one idea your life — think of it, dream of it, live on that idea. Let the brain, muscles, nerves, every part of your body, be full of that idea, and just leave every other idea alone. This is the way to success..." I recommend taking this philosophy and applying it to the work you are doing to help others. By doing this, you will be making a difference!

Making a Difference®

American author and famed motivational speaker John Maxwell said, "Leaders must be close enough to relate to others, but far enough ahead to motivate them." Lead those in your community to change things that need to be altered. Your leadership will make a difference.

_____

_____

_____

_____

_____

_____

_____

_____

_____

_____

_____

_____

_____

_____

_____

_____

_____

_____

_____

_____

Making a Difference®

In making hot tea I opened the box containing Lipton Tea Bags. On the inside cover of the box there was a printed statement, "Why is there a frog on my tea box?" The answer – The Rainforest Alliance Certified seal on the package indicates at least 70% of the tea in the box was grown on Rainforest Alliance Certified tea farms! Lipton is helping protect the environment, improve quality of life and worker welfare. Check it out (liptonforthefuture.com) and see how a well-known tea company is making a difference!

Have you heard of the Negro League Grave Marker Project? It is a project by the Society of American Baseball Research to identify and organize ceremonies to honor former African American players while marking their final resting places. Currently, many of these players, both those well-known and inducted into the Baseball Hall of Fame as well as those not well known, are buried in un-marked graves. This project is attempting to rectify it one grave at a time. Just as these players made a difference to the game of baseball so is the effort to properly recognize them. Thanks to all for working on this project to make a difference!

TIP OF THE DAY

Albert Einstein, the famed scientist, said, "The only source of knowledge is experience." What do you see in your community that you think you cannot fix due to lack of knowledge? Follow Einstein's advice. Get in there and experience working to change things. By doing so, you will be gaining the much desired knowledge and making a difference!

_____

_____

_____

_____

_____

_____

_____

_____

_____

_____

_____

_____

_____

_____

_____

_____

_____

_____

_____

Making a Difference®

2011 marked the 10th anniversary of the 9/11 terrorists attacks on America. A new book worth reading is titled, *You Are With Me Every Day*. It is a book of letters from family members who lost loved ones during that tragic time. Check it out and you will read many stories of how seemingly ordinary things such as a kind word, a dream, a belief, a life made a profound difference!

Former hockey player Wayne Gretzky said, "You miss 100% of the shots you don't take." This statement certainly applies toward efforts to change things. Think about it...if you don't try to change things in your community for others, who will? Take the shot! You don't know what will happen but by trying you will be making a difference!

_____

_____

_____

_____

_____

_____

_____

_____

_____

_____

_____

_____

_____

_____

_____

_____

_____

_____

_____

Making a Difference®

TIP OF THE DAY

Margaret Anderson, the American founder, editor and publisher of *The Little Review*, an art and literary magazine, said, "I have never been able to accept the two great laws of humanity- that you're always being suppressed if you're inspired and always being pushed into the corner if you're exceptional. I won't be cornered and I won't stay suppressed." What are you inspired to do that would be exceptional and ultimately make a difference?

_____

_____

_____

_____

_____

_____

_____

_____

_____

_____

_____

_____

_____

_____

_____

_____

_____

_____

Sister Helen Prejean, who was depicted by Susan Sarandon in the movie *Dead Man Walking*, said, "The important thing is that when you come to understand something you act on it, no matter how small that act is. Eventually it will take you where you need to go." What issue or problem do you understand that you can act on? By doing so, no matter what the size of the act, you will be making a difference!

TIP OF THE DAY

Paul Kuligowski is sixteen (16) and recalls a remarkable moment when he was two (2) years old. Paul said his mother took him to a toy store and told him to a toy store and telling him he could pick any toy but it was not for him. It would be for a child who would not be receiving any gifts for Christmas. That incident caused him to start the Acts of Kindness nonprofit organization that provides essentials such as blankets, diapers, etc. to those in need. Thanks to Paul, and his mom, for making a difference!

_____

_____

_____

_____

_____

_____

_____

_____

_____

_____

_____

_____

_____

_____

_____

_____

Making a Difference®

Do you want to volunteer but don't know where to begin? Check out these websites VolunteerMatch.org or Serve.gov. You can search by your zip code and find opportunities within your own community. By finding a way to volunteer you will be making a difference!

TIP OF THE DAY

The American Community Garden Association (communitygarden.org) has made its mission, through supporting community gardens, to "[improve] people's quality of life by providing a catalyst for neighborhood and community development, stimulating social interaction, encouraging self-reliance, beautifying neighborhoods, producing nutritious food, reducing family food budgets, conserving resources and creating opportunities for recreation, exercise, therapy and education." Check them out and see how you can get involved and truly make a difference.

Making a Difference ®

Charles Orgbon III is fifteen (15) years old and already has made a huge difference in his community of Hoschton, Georgia. He recalls that when he was in the 5th grade, he saw trash and garbage outside his school building and would stay late to pick it up. He often wondered how to make other kids aware of how their actions affected the environment. He is now CEO of Greening Forward which is a nonprofit organization focused on environmental advocacy and education. As of 2011, more than 6,000 students have helped to recycle 10 tons of waste and picking up enough litter to fill 25 homes! Thanks Charles for seeing an opportunity where others only saw a mess. You made a difference!

Have you heard of iGive.com? Through using it to shop, the site will donate up to 26% of your purchases from more than 900 stores to a favorite cause or charity. Check out how shopping can make a difference!

Making a Difference®

I saw an ad in an airline magazine that stated, "What's always the right size, never the wrong color and can't go out of style?" The answer was, "A Donation". Lee Jeans celebrates National Denim Day (the first Monday in October) to fight breast cancer. The ad shares that 1 in 8 women will be diagnosed with breast cancer. Check it out (denimday. com) and see how they are suggesting you give what you would spend on a pair of jeans to fight breast cancer. By participating, you will be making a difference.

Making a Difference®

Annually, Parade magazine recognizes an All-American Service Team. It is amazing what these young people do. Johnny Cohen, 16, from Highland Park, Illinois says he saw a bus moving slowly with lots of exhaust fumes when he was walking home from school in the seventh grade. He asked himself why couldn't the bus be more aerodynamic? Johnny came up with the idea of Green-Shields which is a polycarbonate shield for school buses. This shield decreases pollution, reduces drag and increases mileage! By simply being observant while he was walking home, Johnny Cohen at a young age made a difference!

Making a Difference®

Benjamin McMullen is seventeen (17) years old and from Chesterland, Ohio. He founded two groups to teach children about the environment including area wetlands. He has also created outdoor classrooms at three different schools and built nesting platforms for ospreys while planting 1000 trees. Let's say thank you to a 17 year old who is making a difference in so many ways.

The actress Miranda Cosgrove is better known as the star of Nickelodeon's hit show *iCarly*! In an interview she shared that she believes in the importance of giving back and that, "...everybody can make a difference." Personally, she is an active supporter of St. Jude Children's Research Hospital in Memphis, Tennessee. Thanks to Miranda for making a difference!

Making a Difference®

Have you ever heard of the NFL Alumni Foundation? It is a nonprofit organization whose mission is to serve and support youth oriented charities. Annually hundreds of fundraising, community service and social events are held to raise funds for its Caring for Kids program. Millions of dollars have been raised and contributed benefiting America's youth and various communities. Check it out (nflalumni.org) and see how they live their tagline of "NFL Alumni...Where Legends are Reborn". This group is making a difference!

Making a Difference®

Kids of Courage (kidsoc.org) is a nonprofit organization dedicated to improving the lives of children and young adults with serious illnesses. Their tagline is, "Conquering Illness Through Adventure". On a recent trip, 150 sick and challenged kids traveled across the US to California. With 200 counselors, 17 medical professionals and 30 wheelchairs, these children began an adventure many had never dreamed of...especially as they were going without their parents! Kids of Courage is making a difference in so many ways!

Making a Difference®

What do Dean Martin from "The Ratpack," Fat Tony from "The Simpsons" and David Rossi from "Criminal Minds" have in common? They are all roles played by actor Joe Mantegna. Mantegna has also made it his own role to be a major advocate for charity and giving back to others. He is involved with several organizations advocating for autism research and the protection and enrichment of children. Additionally every Memorial Day, Joe co-hosts with fellow actor Gary Sinise the National Memorial Day Concert broadcast on PBS. Thanks to Joe Mantegna for using your life and talent to make a difference in the lives of others!

I love the writings of poet and novelist Kahlil Gibran. One of my favorites is when he said, "You give but little when you give of your possessions. It is when you give of yourself that you truly give." Think about this and then ponder what you can give of yourself that will make a difference!

_____

_____

_____

_____

_____

_____

_____

_____

_____

_____

_____

_____

_____

_____

_____

_____

_____

_____

_____

_____

Seventeen (17) year old Evan Drucker was born with a birthmark on his face. He wanted to do something to help others in similar situations and to provide information to others. He wrote a book titled *Buddy Booby's Birthmark* whose main character has a birthmark. Since then he has organized an annual read-along to increase tolerance. In 2011, more than 60,000 students participated. Thank you Evan for making a difference!

Making a Difference®

Most of us recall the devastating Japanese earthquake that occurred in 2011. In the cleanup $78 million was found in the rubble. What is amazing is that 85% of this has been returned to its rightful owner. Think about it... devastation and destruction did not dampen the integrity and giving back spirit. The majority of people did the right thing when they found the money and that made all the difference!

Making a Difference®

Have you heard of Hephzibah? It is the oldest charity in Oak Park, Illinois founded by Mary Wessels when in 1897 there was a fire at a nearby orphanage that destroyed it. Upon hearing this, Mary immediately opened her house to these children and then continued to welcome children in her home! Today the services offered by Hephzibah are many but stay true to its mission of caring for society's most vulnerable. Thanks to Mary Wessels for leading the way and making a difference!

Theodore "Teddy" Roosevelt was the 26th President of the United States. He is known for many things including the establishment of the national park system in the United States. Roosevelt made a statement that could be a mantra to live by in the nonprofit world. He said, "Keep your eyes on the stars and your feet on the ground." By doing this, you will be assured of making a difference!

_____

_____

_____

_____

_____

_____

_____

_____

_____

_____

_____

_____

_____

_____

_____

_____

_____

_____

_____

Making a Difference®

While drinking a bottle of water recently, I saw a message on the label. It asked if I had noticed that this bottle had an Eco-Slim Cap. It went on to say it was part of the company's ongoing efforts to reduce their impact on the environment! Thanks to Arrowhead Water for doing their part to help mitigate environmental damage! They are trying to make a difference!

Making a Difference®

In 1940 British Prime Minister Winston Churchill said, "Never in the field of human conflict was so much owed by so many to so few." It referred to the Royal Air Force pilots fighting during the Battle of Britain which they ultimately won delaying the German invasion into Britain. Today, the phrase has been shortened to, "Never was so much owed by so many to so few." What small group could you gather who would do amazing things in your community that would make a difference to many?

_____

_____

_____

_____

_____

_____

_____

_____

_____

_____

_____

_____

_____

_____

_____

_____

_____

Making a Difference®

Famed scientist Albert Einstein is well known for his different way of thinking about science. He once said, "We can't solve problems by using the same kind of thinking we used when we created them." What a profound and true statement! Shake things up; think outside the box. By doing this you might just solve the problem and you will be assured of making a difference!

Making a Difference®

Bill Parcells is a NFL coach who has won two (2) Super Bowls while coaching the New York Giants. He was interviewed for *Harvard Business Review* stating, "In training camps, therefore, we don't focus on the ultimate goal – getting to the Super Bowl. We establish a clear set of goals that are within immediate reach; we're going to be a smart team; we're going to be a well-conditioned team; we're going to be a team that plays hard, etc." What a way to look at making a difference by focusing on immediate steps or goals that will get you to the ultimate goal.

Making a Difference®

I went to purchase a new tube of lipstick at the M.A.C. store. I was informed if I bought a VIVA GLAM lipstick a donation would be made to the M.A.C. Aids Fund (macaidsfund.org). Doing a bit of research, I discovered this company's commitment to, "...serve people of all ages, all races and all sexes affected by HIV and AIDS." Their tagline is "Responsibility is Glamorous". Thanks to the cosmetics company M.A.C. for working every day to make a difference!

Making a Difference®

Many of us have heard of the book *Tuesdays with Morrie* which details the life and death of Morrie Schwartz. Morrie said something that is important to remember when doing work to make a difference. He said, "The most important thing in life is to learn how to give out love, and to let it come in." Whether you are offering help to someone or in need of it, remember to do it with love and you will be making a difference!

_____

_____

_____

_____

_____

_____

_____

_____

_____

_____

_____

_____

_____

_____

_____

_____

_____

_____

Making a Difference®

In 2011, we heard about the Navy SEALs and their work in the world. Have you heard of the Navy SEAL Foundation? Its mission is, "...to provide immediate and ongoing support and assistance to the Naval Special Warfare community and their families." Since 2001, the Navy SEAL Foundation has awarded more than $1.5 million in educational grants to the family members of Navy SEALs. Check it out (navysealfoundation.org) and see how this organization is making a difference!

Making a Difference®

With the advent of e-readers, some people will say we are losing our love of books. However, I would advocate that is not true by simply looking around at the number of book fairs and festivals that take place every year. I recently attended one at the local library in my hometown of Alpena, Michigan with my mom and sister. We were thrilled to walk out with many book "treasures". Books are important. Find the book fair or festival in your community and make a commitment to attend! By doing so, you will be making a difference!

Making a Difference®

Former First Lady Eleanor Roosevelt said, "You must do the thing you think you cannot do." What a powerful mantra to live your life by in terms of being sure you will be making a difference!

_____

_____

_____

_____

_____

_____

_____

_____

_____

_____

_____

_____

_____

_____

_____

_____

_____

_____

_____

_____

_____

Making a Difference®

My friend, Cibeline, is a fashion designer and owned a boutique on Charles Street in Boston. One of the things she commented on is the number of items "stolen" from her store. Every time I heard this, my heart would sink for she worked hard and I find it offensive that someone would take from her! I recently learned through the National Association for Shoplifting Prevention (shopliftingprevention. org) that it is estimated 27 million Americans shoplift each year – that is 1 in 11! Another estimate shows that $35 million worth of goods is stolen every day! Take time to learn how to curb this trend. By gaining information, you will be making a difference!

Making a Difference®

I love shoes! In a magazine, I saw an ad by Nine West. It asked the reader to "Join the Movement." It further stated that Runway Relief Models were raising money for Fashion Targets Breast Cancer. With each step they took in the Runway Relief Boot during the New York City Fashion Week, Nine West was donating $1 per mile walked up to $75,000! Check it out (ninewest.com/runwayrelief) and see how a major shoe company is making a difference.

Making a Difference®

Many parents wonder how to get their children to eat things good for them such as vegetables. Actress Angie Harmon has found a unique way that allows her kids to play with their food then eat it. She shares that during the summer she takes her kids to the farmers' market and encourages them to pick out various vegetables. When they get home they make vegetable pizzas using the veggies to make faces! Onions and carrots can be used for eyebrows and olives for eyeballs with sliced bell peppers being used for the mouths and cherry tomatoes for the noses! Thanks Angie for sharing your clever and fun way to get children to eat their vegetables. You are making a difference!

Making a Difference®

I recently received a thank you note for a donation I made from the Leukemia and Lymphoma Society. The note shared a story that is worth repeating. It said, "Not long ago a contest was held to find the most caring child. The winner was a four (4) year old boy whose neighbor was a lady who had recently lost her daughter to leukemia. Upon seeing her crying, the little boy went into her yard, climbed onto her lap and just sat there. When his mother asked what he had said to the neighbor lady, the little boy replied, "Nothing, I just helped her cry." We all know that little old boy made a difference!

Making a Difference®

Most of us can remember exactly where we were when 9/11 happened. I am still fascinated by the stories of survival and courage. A story that has stayed with me was told by Usman Farman who was a 21 year old Pakistani Muslim when 9/11 occurred. He shared that he had evacuated WTC Building #7 and was told to leave and not look back. With many others he began walking away but did turn to see the first tower collapse and with it a 50 story high wall of dark clouds, debris, glass coming toward him. He began running and fell landing on his back and looking at this massive cloud coming toward him. What amazed him was the person who stopped to help him back to his feet. It was a Hasidic Jewish man who held out his hand and said, "Brother, if you don't mind there is a cloud of glass coming at us, grab my hand and let's get the hell out of here." This is a modern day example of the very familiar Biblical story of the Good Samaritan. Usman never saw this man again but this anonymous person truly made a difference!

_____

_____

_____

_____

_____

_____

_____

Making a Difference®

I am constantly amazed how philanthropy is incorporated into movie and television programs. Recently, I was watching Elvis Presley's first move, *Love Me Tender*. During the old western themed movie, the family attends a picnic with other community members. In the background of a scene, there is a banner that hangs from a partially finished school that says, "Help Build The School House; Buy Something Even If You Don't Need It." I laughed out loud and thought how the opportunity to make a difference is always there!

Making a Difference®

My friend, Marta, forwarded me an article that was titled, "Giving the Gift of You: Being of service to our community is part of being a good citizen of the planet earth." It gave many examples of how you can make a difference by simply giving of yourself including teaching a neighbor kid how to whistle, picking up a piece of trash, not driving your car one day a week, etc. Wonderful ideas for how just being yourself and giving of the gifts you have can make a difference!

Making a Difference®

TIP OF THE DAY

Through the news media we often hear about how economically depressed Michigan and specifically Detroit are these days. But there are groups of people and nonprofit organizations working to make a difference. One of these is Winning Futures (winningfutures.org). This nonprofit organization inspires and prepares youth to succeed through mentoring and life skills programs. This group has not given up on a city and community that many had written off years ago. Winning Futures is working daily to make a difference!

_____

_____

_____

_____

_____

_____

_____

_____

_____

_____

_____

_____

_____

_____

_____

_____

TIP OF THE DAY

The English actress Sarah Alexander said, "The sad truth is that excellence makes people nervous." Don't believe the naysayers and those who say you can't change something. Keep working at it while striving for excellence. You will be making a difference!

_____

_____

_____

_____

_____

_____

_____

_____

_____

_____

_____

_____

_____

_____

_____

_____

_____

_____

_____

_____

Making a Difference®

The author of this quote is unknown but its meaning is powerful. It states, "Excellence can be obtained if you: care more than others think wise; risk more than others think safe; dream more than others think is practical; expect more than others think is possible." This is a great mantra to live by when working to make a difference!

_____

_____

_____

_____

_____

_____

_____

_____

_____

_____

_____

_____

_____

_____

_____

_____

_____

_____

_____

_____

Making a Difference®

In 2007, Rujul Zaparde from New Jersey was 12 years old and on a trip to India. In the villages he saw that women carried pots on their head to get water walking two times a day 1 ½ miles. At that moment he decided he needed to help. He co-founded the non-profit Drinking Water for India (drinkingwaterforindia.org) which as of 2011 had organized 23 schools throughout the United States to pay for 31 water wells in India. Thanks Rujul for making a difference to so many people!

Making a Difference®

Peter Drucker is a famed American author and educator. He said, "Efficiency is doing things right; effectiveness is doing the right things." How true! Are your volunteer efforts efficient or effective? I think we can all agree that being effective makes a difference!

Riders for Health (riders.org) joined ABC News and the United Nations Foundation in their Million Moms Challenge. According to the press release, "This first-of-its kind initiative will connect millions of Americans with millions of moms in developing countries around the world to engage on the critical issues of pregnancy, childbirth and children's health--moms here helping moms worldwide." Thanks to all three (3) organizations for working together to make a difference!

Making a Difference®

I saw my friend Billy McLaughlin (billymclaughlin. com) perform in Chicago. He is an amazing guitar player who at the height of his career started missing notes in concert to songs he had composed and played for years. He couldn't figure out what was wrong. After many visits to doctors and clinics he was diagnosed with focal dystonia (dystonia-foundation.org) which eliminated use of his right hand. So he did an amazing thing – he learned how to play left-handed! Check it out and see how Billy, who is now a spokesperson for dystonia awareness, is making a difference!

TIP OF THE DAY

Have you heard of Eric F. Ross? He fled Nazi Germany in 1938 but returned as a US soldier in 1942 with a group of others known as the "Ritchie Boys" because they spoke German. He survived and always remembered what he had witnessed firsthand! At his death, he left a $17.2 million gift to the US Holocaust Memorial Museum, the largest single gift ever received by them! Eric and his wife, Lore, definitely made a difference and helped insure we will never forget what happened!

Apple Co-Founder Steve Jobs made a difference in many ways. Did you know his philanthropy was often done anonymously? In 2005 he said, "Remembering that you are going to die is the best way I know to avoid the trap of thinking you have something to lose." A good mantra to live by to insure that you will do things in your life and community to make a difference!

_____

_____

_____

_____

_____

_____

_____

_____

_____

_____

_____

_____

_____

_____

_____

_____

_____

_____

_____

_____

TIP OF THE DAY

Walt Disney said, "The way to get started is to quit talking and begin doing." Great advice for how to make a difference in your community!

_____

_____

_____

_____

_____

_____

_____

_____

_____

_____

_____

_____

_____

_____

_____

_____

_____

_____

_____

_____

_____

_____

_____

_____

Making a Difference®

TIP OF THE DAY

Thomas Paine was a pivotal figure in the American Revolutionary War penning *Common Sense*, the pamphlet that became a best seller that supported America's independence from Great Britain. He said, "I love the man that can smile in trouble, that can gather strength from distress, and grow brave by reflection." Imagine if you chose to live by this message. What could you do in your community by adopting this attitude? You would definitely be making a difference!

_____

_____

_____

_____

_____

_____

_____

_____

_____

_____

_____

_____

_____

_____

_____

_____

Making a Difference®

Did you know that it is estimated that annually 160 million tons of home improvement waste go to landfills? Have you hear of Diggers List? Created by Matt Knox and Johnnie Munger, DiggersList (diggerslist.com) was founded in 2009 as a place where people could buy and sell leftover building materials. Things such as barn board or restored chandeliers are available through the 34 different categories a visitor can peruse. There is no cost to posting an ad and there is an option to convert your sale item into a donation offer. Thanks to Matt and Johnnie for thinking outside the box and making a difference!

_____

_____

_____

_____

_____

_____

_____

_____

_____

_____

_____

_____

_____

Making a Difference®

One of America's most famous inventors, Thomas Edison, said, "Many of life's failures are men who did not realize how close they were to success when they gave up." What a profound statement! What are you about to give up on? Does it affect your community? Spend some time today thinking about what could happen if you did not give up. What success might be found if you just keep working to make a difference?

_____

_____

_____

_____

_____

_____

_____

_____

_____

_____

_____

_____

_____

_____

_____

_____

_____

Making a Difference®

The Daniel Murphy Scholarship Foundation was started in 1989 by ten (10) business associates in Chicago. Their idea was to enrich the lives of youth in Chicago by providing them educational opportunities they probably would not have access to otherwise. More than 20 years later, 75-100 scholarships are given to 8th graders annually. Think about it...ten people came together with an idea and that idea lead to an effort that is still making a difference!

Making a Difference®

I have found that old saying "It is better to give than receive" is really true! If you were asked to name your favorite nonprofit organization, could you? What really touches your heart? To which charitable endeavors do you give your money and time? Take time today to think about these questions and your answers. This is the beginning of your planning for your year-end philanthropic efforts to make a difference!

_____

_____

_____

_____

_____

_____

_____

_____

_____

_____

_____

_____

_____

_____

_____

_____

_____

Making a Difference®

Famed American architect Frank Lloyd Wright said, "The truth is more important than the facts." What truth is facing you about something in your community? Follow the advice of the architect; disregard the facts that say something can't be done and follow the truth of what is possible. By doing this, you will be making a difference!

Making a Difference®

My childhood friend Marcy sent a request to each of her friends in anticipation of her 50th birthday. She asked each of us to try to do something each week to help someone else and to let her know. Marcy let us know she had asked 50 friends and if we each did it there would be more than 2500 acts of kindness occurring! One person asking fifty (50) friends to do something to change the world each week. You can be assured that Marcy and her friends will be making a difference!

_____

_____

_____

_____

_____

_____

_____

_____

_____

_____

_____

_____

_____

_____

_____

_____

_____

_____

Making a Difference®

Most hotels these days have begun to pay attention to being "green". You can usually find a sign or placard in the bathroom stating that in an effort to reduce the thousands of gallons of water and detergent used each year you can help by re-using your towel. A simple idea but a powerful way to make a difference!

_____

_____

_____

_____

_____

_____

_____

_____

_____

_____

_____

_____

_____

_____

_____

_____

_____

_____

_____

_____

_____

_____

Do you shut the lights off when you leave a room? I remember my parents telling us to do this when I was a child. It was an easy way to reduce the energy bill my family received monthly. Nowadays it is a habit I am resurrecting in order to reduce my carbon footprint. What can you do to change your habits and reduce your carbon footprint? Consider unplugging your phone chargers and small appliances when they are not in use; shut off lights when you leave a room; turn down the heat in your home. All of these seemingly small efforts will make a difference!

_____

_____

_____

_____

_____

_____

_____

_____

_____

_____

_____

_____

_____

_____

_____

_____

_____

Making a Difference®

French author, journalist and philosopher Albert Camus said, "Real generosity towards the future lies in giving all to the present." Today give your attention to those things you can do right now that will begin the change needed in your community for the future. Your attention to the present will make a difference!

Making a Difference®

Nineteenth Century English writer Arthur
Helps said, "Wise sayings often fall on barren ground, but a kind word is never thrown away." This is so true! How often have you tried to remember a quote you love but find it difficult? Now think about the kind words spoken to you and how easily you remember these. Kind words are a gift! Speak kind words today to everyone! This gift is easy to give and definitely makes a difference!

Making a Difference®

Friday is the day a lot of people look forward to all week. However, every day can be that. Today, make it a point to do something nice for someone else...perhaps pause a minute to hold open a door, put money in an expired meter, let someone cut (i.e., merge) in front of you on the highway or simply acknowledge all you meet with a bright smile and a joyous hello! You will be amazed how your actions and attitude make a difference!

Making a Difference®

Walt Disney had a great vision. However it is said before his success he failed at least seven (7) times in his initial business endeavors. He is quoted as saying, "It's kind of fun to do the impossible." What a powerful statement! What seems impossible in your community to accomplish? Why not change your attitude and have fun with what seems impossible? You just might make a lasting difference!

_____

_____

_____

_____

_____

_____

_____

_____

_____

_____

_____

_____

_____

_____

_____

_____

_____

_____

Frederick William Robertson

was a 19th century English preacher who said, "To believe is to be strong. Doubt cramps energy. Belief is power." These are amazing words to live by. Believe. Be powerful. Make a difference!

Making a Difference®

Nelson Mandela said, "After climbing a great hill, one only finds that there are many more hills to climb. I have taken a moment here to rest, to steal a view of the glorious vista that surrounds me, to look back on the distance I have come." Even though we are all busy trying to get things accomplished, take a moment to rest and look back. To realize what you have done to change things! This might be the best thing you do to make a difference in your life.

American social writer and author Eric Hoffer said, "There can be no real freedom without the freedom to fail." Feel free to fail today even as you try to make a difference. It is the getting up and trying again that really makes a difference!

Making a Difference®

I picked up a promotional marketing piece at the offices of the American Red Cross of Greater New York. It read, "Do Great Things Every Day! Volunteer!" What a powerful invitation to remind us how easy it can be to make a difference!

Have you heard of The Doe Network (doe-network.org)? According to their website their mission is, "... devoted to assisting law enforcement in solving cold cases concerning unexplained disappearances and unidentified victims from North America, Australia and Europe. It is our mission to give the nameless back their names and return the missing to their families. We hope to accomplish this mission in three ways; by giving the cases exposure on our website, by having our volunteers search for clues on these cases as well as making possible matches between missing and unidentified persons and lastly through attempting to get media exposure for these cases that need and deserve it." Thank you to the Doe Network for caring and working to make a difference in very difficult situations.

Making a Difference®

I am often asked what impact I think the ability to take a tax deduction for a charitable donation has on a person's desire to give. My answer often surprises people as I say, very little. Survey after survey shows that only 6-8% of people say that a tax deduction is their primary motivation in making their charitable decisions. Americans give because they want to make a difference!

TIP OF THE DAY

I read this quote and thought it profound. It states, "There are always two choices. Two paths to take. One is easy. And its only reward is that it's easy." Choose today to take the path that might change things in your community. It might not be the easy path but it will make a difference!

_____

_____

_____

_____

_____

_____

_____

_____

_____

_____

_____

_____

_____

_____

_____

_____

_____

_____

_____

Making a Difference®

Harry Belafonte is a well-known singer, songwriter, actor and yes, social activist. In 2011 on the MSNBC show *Morning Joe*, he was asked by the hosts why he personally bankrolled Dr. Martin Luther King, Jr. and those working for civil rights. His response was profound. He said, "I could have bought more homes in Hollywood with pools and tried to backstroke my way to the bank or I could help change the world." Thanks Harry for in such a simple way stating the truth...that making a difference always affects change in the world.

Many wonder why people choose to work in the nonprofit field often citing the perceived lack of "making a money" as one reason they would not do it. I like what famed entrepreneur Walt Disney said, "You reach a point where you don't work for money." I think he meant that when you do what you love you don't work for money but for something else. In the nonprofit world, many employees don't work for money but work because they know their efforts make a difference!

_____

_____

_____

_____

_____

_____

_____

_____

_____

_____

_____

_____

_____

_____

_____

_____

Making a Difference®

When I see news coverage of missing people, usually women, it always breaks my heart. I wonder what happened to them. Where did they go? Will they be found? One only has to think of the coverage that followed Lacy Peterson, Natalie Hollaway and baby Lisa Irwin to recall those reporters sharing with all us the findings. What is amazing is how little news coverage people of color receive when they are reported as missing. The Black and Missing Foundation (blackandmissinginc.com) is working to change this. Their mission is to bring awareness to missing persons of color. Check it out. The work they do is making a difference!

I love hearing stories about class reunions. I enjoy learning how they bring people together, heal old wounds and begin new friendships. My mom recently attended her 50th class reunion and told me a story about a found yearbook. It seemed a classmate's husband was at a garage sale and saw a yearbook from his wife's school and class year. He opened it and saw that it was inscribed and signed to a classmate named "Mike". For fifty cents, he bought the yearbook and at the reunion he gave it to "Mike". Mike was stunned. He had not seen his yearbook in 50 years saying that his mother had given it away years ago with a box of books. What a difference curiosity and fifty cents made! What could you be curious about or do that is seemingly simply but would make a difference?

_____

_____

_____

_____

_____

_____

_____

_____

_____

_____

_____

_____

Making a Difference®

Famed playwright William Shakespeare, often called simply The Bard, is credited with stating, "There is nothing either good or bad, but thinking makes it so." By simply changing your thinking, you will make a difference!

_____

_____

_____

_____

_____

_____

_____

_____

_____

_____

_____

_____

_____

_____

_____

_____

_____

_____

_____

_____

_____

_____

Making a Difference ®

Actor Mark Wahlberg started a foundation in May 2011 named as you might expect "The Mark Wahlberg Youth Foundation". He joined forces with the Taco Bell Foundation For Teens to address the teen dropout rate from high school. Did you know that in 1 in 3 students drop out of high school? Mark Wahlberg along with Taco Bell is trying to do something about this and ultimately make a difference!

TIP OF THE DAY

While there is debate whether William A. Foster or William F. Foster said this, it is a powerful statement to consider. "Quality is never an accident; it is always the result of high intention, sincere effort, intelligent direction and skillful execution. It represents the wise choice of many alternatives." Think about this. Working with quality as a goal always makes a difference in whatever you are doing!

Making a Difference®

In 2003, Bob Thompson wanted to change public education in Detroit. The multi-millionaire philanthropist offered the city $200 million to build 15 charter high schools. The offer was rejected and Thompson, a road builder, took his money offer off the table. In 2011, Detroit Mayor David Bing made a phone call and asked Bob and his wife, Ellen, to lunch. During that lunch he said that children in Detroit deserved another opportunity at having a quality education. After their first endeavor to try to change things they were not sure what could be done but after lunch, Mr. Thompson said, "He convinced Ellen and I that we should re-engage in the city and make a difference." The result is a $16.5 million college preparatory charter high school in Detroit's Rivertown! An offer, a lunch and an opportunity to change the world! Thanks to Bob and Ellen, as well as Mayor Bing, for seeing the possibilities to make a difference!

Making a Difference®

Did you know the Big Brothers Big Sisters (BBBS) national organization has a special Military Mentoring program for children with parents in the armed services? BBBS pairs children with adults who are serving in the military as well as veterans and civilians. Check it out (bbbs.org) and see how this nonprofit organization is making a difference!

_____

_____

_____

_____

_____

_____

_____

_____

_____

_____

_____

_____

_____

_____

_____

_____

_____

_____

_____

_____

_____

Making a Difference®

Have you heard of the nonprofit Homes for Our Troops? It works to construct houses for severely injured veterans who have served in the military after 9/11. Check it out (homesforourtroops.org) and consider making a financial donation, donating equipment or helping to build a home. By doing any one of these things you will be making a difference to those who have given a great sacrifice for our country!

Making a Difference®

Did you know the D.A.V. (Disabled American Veterans) provides free transportation to men and women who are not able to travel to VA medical facilities and hospitals? You can help by offering to drive a DAV van for those who need assistance. Check it out (dav.org/volunteers) and see how easy it is to make a difference!

TIP OF THE DAY

Have you ever thought about what happens to pets when a soldier is deployed or returns injured and is unable to care for the animal? Consider becoming a foster care provider to a pet. Check it out (guardianangelsfor-soldierspet.org) and see how you can make a difference to those who are or have made a huge difference for our country!

_____

_____

_____

_____

_____

_____

_____

_____

_____

_____

_____

_____

_____

_____

_____

_____

_____

_____

_____

Making a Difference®

The Library of Congress (LOC) is on a mission and needs your help! The LOC wants to record the voices of old soldiers telling their stories. Do you know an old soldier from the front line with a tale to tell? Check out how easy it is to conduct an interview (loc.gov/vets). By conducting an interview and recording a story you will be making a difference!

Making a Difference®

Do you have a drawer or box filled with old cell phones? Do you want to do something special with them? Consider donating them to Cell Phones for Soldiers. For each one donated, the organization will pay for one hour of talk time for troops deployed overseas. Check it out (cellphonesforsoldiers.com) and see how easy it is to make a difference!

Making a Difference®

I love clipping coupons and the fun of saving money! Did you know military families can use them for up to six months past their expiration date? Instead of throwing out your old coupons, use them for good. Check it out (coupsfortroops.com) and see how your coupon clipping can make a difference!

Making a Difference®

Actor George Clooney travels to Sudan in Africa many times in an attempt to draw attention to the conditions there after the civil war that had lasted for decades. When asked why he got involved, he said, "I wasn't going to stand on the sidelines and not participate." He cited that two million people had been killed in the north-south war in Sudan before 2005. George Clooney by saying it simply and getting involved is making a difference!

Making a Difference®

Many of us recall the movie *The Blind Side* which detailed the life of Michael Oher and his adoption by Sean and Leigh Anne Touhy. In 2011, another book of kindness similar to this was published. The name of the book is *The Invisible Thread* and tells the story of a chance encounter on a Manhattan sidewalk in 1986 of Laura Schroff, a successful newspaper executive, and Maurice Mazyck, an eleven (11) year old skinny kid. Maurice was hungry and asked Laura for change. Instead of simply continuing her pace, the 37 year old turned around and took Maurice to McDonald's for a Big Mac, fries and a chocolate shake. It was the beginning of a 25 year friendship that changed both of their lives. They now tell their story and if you read it, you will see how easy it can be to begin making a difference!

Have you heard of Veterans Farm? It is located west of Jacksonville, Florida and was started by US Army Sergeant Adam Burke. Injured in Iraq, the former star high school athlete decided to return to his parents' farm with his wife. His family gave him 2½ acres. Using his disability benefits he bought blueberry bushes and irrigation equipment. Now, with assistance from the Work Vessels for Veterans (wvfv.net) nonprofit organization, he bought more land. Today other veterans come to his farm to regain some of what they have lost. The farm is a source of comfort for many. A simple idea of returning to one's roots that is making a difference for so many!

Making a Difference®

What would you do if you bought a house with all its contents and found $23,800 under the bed in a bag? Would you keep it? That was the test facing Cathy Ward and her husband, Joe DeGreif. They had purchased a 1940s white frame house with all its furnishings from the family of an elderly woman who had died. As they sat and counted the money, which would have paid off their debt and allowed them to make the improvements needed to the house, they pondered this question. Then they did what I suspect most of us would do. They returned the money to the woman's stunned family. Thank you to Cathy and Joe for showing us all how to make a difference!!

Making a Difference®

Many nonprofit organizations

own and operate thrift stores. I always try to shop at them and found the one run by the Espanola Valley Animal Shelter (evalleyshelter.org) in Santa Fe especially full of great finds. I find it most appropriate to appreciate all those who donate items that consumers like me buy. By working together we all are making a difference!

Making a Difference®

I love the kindness of strangers when they hear or read about a need! A story about a grave headstone that was purchased but not delivered by a company led readers of the *Chicago Tribune* to come to the rescue insuring a headstone for Narciso Paredes is in place. This is only one example of daily occurrences of random kindness. All of which I believe make a difference!

Making a Difference®

TIP OF THE DAY

Most of us at one time have watched a *Law and Order* episode. My favorite series is the *Law and Order: Special Victims Unit* series which features Mariska Hagitay. If you notice, she often wears two necklaces, one that was designed by MeandRo for her Joyful Heart Foundation (joyfulheartfoundation.org). This nonprofit organization helps survivors of sexual assault, domestic violence and child abuse. Thanks to Mariska for her outstanding work in the series and for taking time to make a difference!

182

Making a Difference®

I saw an advertisement in a magazine in which country music artist, singer and songwriter Brad Paisley was pictured with a guitar in one hand and holding up his index finger on the other hand. The ad said, "Free to play to sing to speak to write." It was a statement sharing that because of the First Amendment we all can be whoever and whatever we want to be. Check it out (1forall.us) and take a stand for the First Amendment. You will be making a difference!

183

Making a Difference®

Many celebrities use their "star" power to highlight an issue or start a nonprofit organization. Brad Pitt is no exception. After Hurricane Katrina, he focused his efforts on constructing new green houses for the victims in New Orleans. Through the efforts of the Make It Right Foundation (makeitrightnola.org) Brad Pitt and many others saw a need and opportunity to lead them to make a difference!

TIP OF THE DAY

Former Chicago Mayor Joseph Medill took office soon after the Great Fire of 1871. He was responsible for the reconstruction and building of Chicago after the devastating fire that was allegedly started by Mrs. O'Leary's cow (the cow has since been exonerated)! To help fund the reconstruction, Medill sought donations and gifts in the amount of $5 million from donors throughout the world as well as working with the federal government to rebate import taxes on construction materials. He also created the city's first public library which was needed to house the myriad of donated books sent from England. Mayor Medill made a difference as did many others who made donations!

Making a Difference®

Music Saves Lives (musicsaveslives.org) is a nonprofit organization founded in 2005. Its mission is to serve as the bridge between music and important lifesaving causes. Check it out and see how this group of people is making a difference!

The best-selling author, sportswriter and philanthropist Mitch Albom said, "The way you get meaning into your life is to devote yourself to loving others, devote yourself to your community around you, and devote yourself to creating something that gives you purpose and meaning." Mitch definitely has shown his devotion in Detroit, Michigan where he has founded four (4) charities. What will you devote yourself to today to help make a difference?

_____

_____

_____

_____

_____

_____

_____

_____

_____

_____

_____

_____

_____

_____

_____

_____

_____

_____

Making a Difference®

We often learn about the misdeeds of celebrities when they do something wrong, but what about when they do something good? According to the Giving Back Fund's 2011 list of famous philanthropists, here are some celebrities doing good. Actress Jami Gertz and her husband Tony Ressler donated more than $10.5 million to charitable causes. Famed musician Herb Alpert donated more than $9 million and actor Mel Gibson donated more than $6.8 million. Film maker George Lucas gave away more than $4.25 million and rounding out the top five list is author Nora Roberts who donated $3 million. These six (6) individuals gave away more than $33 million and most certainly made a difference!

Making a Difference®

What do the movies *Forest Gump, Braveheart* and *Titanic* have in common? The answer is film executive Sherry Lansing who was the first woman to head a studio when she assumed the lead of 20th Century Fox. Even though she spent her career in California and Hollywood she didn't forget her roots and in 2011 donated $5 million to the University of Chicago Lab Schools' $55 million campaign. Sherry Lansing, a pioneer in film and now a leader in a fundraising campaign by providing almost 10% of the overall goal with one gift, is definitely making a difference!

I recently read the story about a game of chess and how it forged a friendship. Now this might not seem strange except the friendship was formed between Shawn Hu, an immigration attorney who works in downtown Chicago, and Alexander Pinkston, a homeless man who sleeps outside the building next to the one in which Shawn works. It seems that while Shawn had noticed him, it was Andrew's playing chess that intrigued him and became the catalyst for a friendship born out of playing the game. Andrew beat Shawn the first day and for quite a few days after until he finally taught Shawn his winning move: how to get to checkmate with a king and a rook. Two men from very different backgrounds formed a friendship through the game of chess. What game could you play today that would make a difference in someone else's life?

_____

_____

_____

_____

_____

_____

_____

_____

_____

_____

You often hear we are now living in a global world without barriers. However living in the United States, an English speaking country, it is often easy to forget there are other languages. For example, did you know that 500 million people in the world speak Spanish? Why not take time to learn another language whether it be Spanish, French, Chinese, Swahili or Sign. By doing this you will be making a difference in your world and most likely a difference for others as well.

_____

_____

_____

_____

_____

_____

_____

_____

_____

_____

_____

_____

_____

_____

_____

_____

_____

Making a Difference®

American television and radio personality Larry Elder said, "A goal without a plan is just a wish." What is your wish for your community or your life? Ask yourself what is the real goal and then work toward a plan. It is by making this plan that you will be assured of making a difference!

_____

_____

_____

_____

_____

_____

_____

_____

_____

_____

_____

_____

_____

_____

_____

_____

_____

_____

_____

_____

Making a Difference®

Albert Pike lived in the 1800s and was an American lawyer, soldier and journalist. He said, "What we have done for ourselves alone dies with us; what we have done for others and the world remains and is immortal." How very true! Today, do something for someone else or for something in your community. You can be assured you will be making a difference that will last and perhaps even be immortal!

Making a Difference®

In 1963 in more than 75 newspapers you could be assured you would read a one-panel cartoon titled, *The Country Parson*, by Frank A. Clark and receive a powerful and often weighty message. One of my favorites is, "If you can find a path with no obstacles, it probably doesn't lead anywhere." How true! When trying to change things you will encounter roadblocks, stubborn people, naysayers, etc. Don't stop. Keep going. By doing this you will be making a difference!

Making a Difference®

In an interview in the 1980s, Frank A. Clark, author of the one-panel cartoon titled *The Country Parson* said, "...most of the good things that have happened to me in my career happened by accident when I was trying to help someone else." Powerful words to live by and a seemingly guaranteed way to make a difference!

_____

_____

_____

_____

_____

_____

_____

_____

_____

_____

_____

_____

_____

_____

_____

_____

_____

_____

_____

_____

_____

Making a Difference®

Have you heard of the restaurant chain Panera Bread Bakery-Cafes? There are more than 1500 of them operating through the US. Since its founding, giving has been a critical part of the corporation. For more than ten (10) years the company has been giving back locally through donations of cash or donations of bakery products at the end of the day. The total is $150-200 million worth of food and another $2 million through the collection boxes at each store in which customers make donations, usually from their change that is then supplemented by Panera annually! Panera Bread is making a difference!

_____

_____

_____

_____

_____

_____

_____

_____

_____

_____

_____

_____

_____

_____

Marian Tompson is a true pioneer! She is one of the seven (7) women who founded the LaLeche League (llli.org) in the late 1950s when the norm was for new moms to not breast feed their newborns. At the time it was very controversial, but this group of women changed the course of feeding babies. What is remarkable is that Marian picked up the charge again and founded another nonprofit organization called Another Look (anotherlook. org) which challenges scientists and researchers to take "another look" at breast feeding and HIV/Aids to see if there really is a link (meaning can the virus be passed from mom to newborn or are anitbodies passed). In third world and developing countries, often the only source of nutrition for newborns and children is breast milk (meaning infant formula is not available). Marian is a courageous woman who is challenging us to consider thinking differently about the assumed connection. She is doing something others were afraid to do and that has made all the difference!

Making a Difference®

Mario Cuomo, the former governor of the state of New York, said, "I talk and talk and talk, and I haven't taught people in 50 years what my father taught by example in one week." Let your actions teach today! Lead by example! You will be making a difference!

_____

_____

_____

_____

_____

_____

_____

_____

_____

_____

_____

_____

_____

_____

_____

_____

_____

_____

_____

_____

Making a Difference®

Famed actress Lauren Bacall said, "I think your whole life shows in your face and you should be proud of that." What is your face showing today? Does is show how you have or have tried to make a difference in your world?

_____

_____

_____

_____

_____

_____

_____

_____

_____

_____

_____

_____

_____

_____

_____

_____

_____

_____

_____

_____

_____

_____

_____

Making a Difference®

In 2011, I saw bright yellow banners in downtown Chicago saying Go Do Good. It is an effort to turn art into action encouraging Chicagoans to do 100,000 good deeds over the summer! The focus in June was helping kids read, in July to help kids get healthy and in August assisting kids in getting ready for school. Check it out (godogood.org) and see how the Chicagoans worked to make a difference!

Former first lady Eleanor Roosevelt said, "What one has to do usually can be done." What do you see in your life or community that "needs to be done"? Follow Eleanor Roosevelt's advice and see how it makes a difference in your attitude and what you can accomplish.

_____

_____

_____

_____

_____

_____

_____

_____

_____

_____

_____

_____

_____

_____

_____

_____

_____

_____

_____

_____

Martin Luther King, Jr. said, "The heart of the giver makes the gift dear and precious." Where is your heart focused? Is it on doing what you can to make a difference every day?

_____

_____

_____

_____

_____

_____

_____

_____

_____

_____

_____

_____

_____

_____

_____

_____

_____

_____

_____

_____

_____

Making a Difference®

Anais Nin was a French-Cuban author who said, "Each friend represents a world in us, a world possibly not born until they arrive, and it is only by this meeting that a new world is born." These are profound words to live by. Make a new friend today; see the new world and opportunities that are born. By doing this one seemingly simple act, you will be making a difference in your life and the lives of others.

TIP OF THE DAY

Being in the philanthropy business I am often asked, especially by my mom, how I can "beg" or ask people for money every day. My answer is always, "I don't beg people for money, I give them the opportunity to change the world." Donating money changes things and does make a difference!

_____

_____

_____

_____

_____

_____

_____

_____

_____

_____

_____

_____

_____

_____

_____

_____

_____

_____

_____

_____

TIP OF THE DAY

𝒮eventeenth century famed philosopher Francis Bacon said, "Money is like manure, not good except when it is spread." Words said 400 years ago that are still relevant today. Annually set a charitable budget and then implement it. Donate money to the causes you care about and see how you will make a difference!

_____

_____

_____

_____

_____

_____

_____

_____

_____

_____

_____

_____

_____

_____

_____

_____

_____

_____

_____

Making a Difference®

Did you know it is reported 60% of people living in institutions don't receive visitors, especially over the holidays. Make it a point to take time to visit a care facility near your home or office that houses people who are elderly or might have a disability. By simply making this commitment, you will be making a difference!

_____

_____

_____

_____

_____

_____

_____

_____

_____

_____

_____

_____

_____

_____

_____

_____

_____

_____

_____

_____

TIP OF THE DAY

$\mathcal{F}$amed pioneer settlement worker, philosopher, sociologist and the founder of Hull House, Jane Addams, said, "Nothing could be worse than the fear that one had given up too soon and left one unexpended effort that might have saved the world." I wholeheartedly agree! Don't give up too soon. Keep working to make a difference every day!

TIP OF THE DAY

Have you heard of the nationwide effort called Project Linus (www.projectlinus.com)? It is named for the "Linus" character from the very popular Peanuts comic strip that always carried a blanket. Its mission is to accept new, homemade blankets to distribute to needy children. It is a simple project with the ability and opportunity to make a profound difference to many!

Annually, the United States celebrates

Independence Day on July 4th, the day the Declaration of Independence was signed. One doesn't have to be a great lover of history to realize that the Founding Fathers (and Mothers) had a pretty good idea when they decided to put their faith in a free county as well as their fortunes and in some cases their lives! These "revolutionaries" definitely made a difference! And by declaring our independence in many ways, this decision led directly to the creation of the nonprofit/philanthropic sector because there wasn't a king or queen to provide support for hospitals, libraries, schools, churches, poor houses, etc. The colonists in signing their names to that document in essence created the nonprofit sector in which more than 12 million of us work (that is 9% of the work force) today! Thanks to our Founders for making a difference!

Making a Difference®

John Andrew Holmes was an American clergyman and one of the leaders of the Social Gospel Movement in 20th Century American Protestantism. He said and I agree, "There is no exercise better for the heart than reaching down and lifting people up." Do your part today to exercise today and see how you make a difference!

TIP OF THE DAY

Famed French-Cuban author Anais Nin said, "We don't see things are they are, we see them as we are." How very true. Change or alter your perspective today about something in your community or world. It will make a difference!

_____

_____

_____

_____

_____

_____

_____

_____

_____

_____

_____

_____

_____

_____

_____

_____

_____

_____

_____

Making a Difference®

Mission Men is a ten (10) year old program of the nonprofit organization Family Focus. Located on Chicago's west side, it has a simple mission - to help men become better dads. Men from different parts of the city and region as well as differing backgrounds meet to learn how to make changes in their lives and to have a better relationship with their children. With eight (8) locations throughout the Chicagoland area, Mission Men is making a difference!

_____

_____

_____

_____

_____

_____

_____

_____

_____

_____

_____

_____

_____

_____

_____

_____

_____

_____

_____

TIP OF THE DAY

Author Paul J. Meyer said, "Ninety percent of all those who fail are not actually defeated. They simply quit." Don't quit. Keep working to make a difference every day!

_____

_____

_____

_____

_____

_____

_____

_____

_____

_____

_____

_____

_____

_____

_____

_____

_____

_____

_____

_____

_____

_____

Walt Disney said, "A person should set his goals as early as he can and devote all his energy and talent to getting there. With enough effort, he may achieve it. Or he may find something that is even more rewarding. But in the end, no matter what the outcome, he will know he has been alive." A powerful statement that I recommend every one consider for their personal mantra. By following this advice, you know you will be making a difference!

Former US Senator and Presidential Candidate Hubert Humphrey said, "This, then, is the test we must set for ourselves; not to march alone but to march in such a way that others will wish to join us." Do you see something in your family, community or the world that needs to be changed? Start something today and work in such a way that others will want to join you and lend their efforts to the change you are trying to bring about. By leading in this manner, you will be assured that you are making a difference!

Making a Difference®

TIP OF THE DAY

Have you heard of the Asirvadh Children's Home located in Thiruvallur, India? A LMDA Associate visited it in 2011 and discovered how they support a large number of underprivileged women and children in India in need of hope for a better life. It was founded in 1994 by a woman named Jeyanthi Asheervath who decided she had to do something about this great need for those marginalized in India. Check it out (asirvadhashram.com) and see how one person can start something that makes a difference to so many!

TIP OF THE DAY

Seventeenth century English military man and politician Oliver Cromwell said, "He who stops being better stops being good." Keep working at being better which leads to being good and ultimately to making a difference.

_____

_____

_____

_____

_____

_____

_____

_____

_____

_____

_____

_____

_____

_____

_____

_____

_____

_____

_____

_____

_____

Making a Difference®

Many of us grew up on Kraft Macaroni and Cheese as well as other Kraft products including Fig Newtons, Corn-Nuts, Crystal Light, A-1 Steak Sauce and the list goes on and on. But I am wondering if you knew more than 30,000 Kraft employees volunteer annually in outreach programs in hundreds of communities throughout the US and in more than 60 countries? Kraft and its employees work daily to make a difference in what they create for our tables and what they do in our communities!

TIP OF THE DAY

Mother Teresa said, "We ourselves feel that what we are doing is just a drop in the ocean. But the ocean would be less because of that missing drop." Don't be less than what you can be. Do what you have to do to make a difference!

Making a Difference®

TIP OF THE DAY

I read an interview conducted with Brad Pitt in 2011. In it he was asked by the reporter how he and Angelina Jolie find time to help refugees and other victims all over the world and why. He responded by saying, "I'll tell you why: I hit the lottery – the whole cliché of moving to Hollywood and getting paid silly amounts of money. I've traveled the world and seen mothers and babies dying because they don't have a 30 cent treatment that is available in industrialized nations. I feel like I have to share whatever I can. You're culpable if you don't act." Profound words from an actor who knows how to make a difference!

Making a Difference®

The Panera Bread Bakery-Café chain recently opened up three (3) stores called Panera Cares. The twist is that if you are unable to pay the regular or usual price for something on the menu, you are allowed to pay what you can. They have suggested donation levels with some customers paying more than the listed price. Panera Bread is committed to all the residents of a community, even those with limited means. This company is definitely making a difference!

_____

_____

_____

_____

_____

_____

_____

_____

_____

_____

_____

_____

_____

_____

Making a Difference®

John Wooden, former UCLA basketball coach and one of the greatest coaches of all time, said, "When you improve a little each day, eventually big things occur....Don't look for the quick, big improvement. Seek the small improvement one day at a time. That's the only way it happens – and when it happens, it lasts." What a way to consider making a difference...small improvements daily!

Have you seen the magazine ads featuring elephants? The caption says, "Be the voice for those who have no voice." It's an invitation to join the World Wildlife Federation (worldwildlife.org). Check it out and see how you can make a difference!

Making a Difference®

Every 26 seconds a student drops out of high school. When I first heard this statistic I was startled and alarmed. Then I thought, what can I do to stop this cycle? Think about what you can do today to change the direction of a student who might be considering ending his or her high school education early. Do something today to make a difference!

Making a Difference®

Have you heard of Connor Dantzler? He is a seventeen (17) year old from Maryland who created an organization called Health through Humor (healththrough-humor.com). It seems when he was eight (8) years old he wanted to volunteer but no organization would take him because of his young age. He decided he wanted to bring joy to people so he thought about bringing joy to sick people. Today, his organization has distributed more than 11,000 joke books to hospitals located in nineteen (19) states! Talk about making a difference!

Making a Difference®

Did you know that 1 in 88 military children have been diagnosed with autism? ACT Today! For Military Families (ATMF), is a branch of Autism Care and Treatment. It is a nonprofit organization creating opportunities of support and care for these children. The donations of concerned citizens help already burdened military families access effective treatment and support. Go to the website (acttoday-formilitaryfamilies.org) to read about how ATMF has made a difference and learn how you can contribute to helping America's military families facing autism.

_____

_____

_____

_____

_____

_____

_____

_____

_____

_____

_____

_____

_____

_____

Making a Difference®

John Wayne, the famous actor and director, said, "Tomorrow is the most important thing in life. Comes into us at midnight very clean. It's perfect when it arrives and it puts itself in our hands. It hopes we've learned something from yesterday." Think about the opportunity each day presents us to make a difference!

Making a Difference®

Most of us have heard of the Ronald McDonald Houses. Did you know they were first established in 1974? Kim Hill, daughter of former Philadelphia Eagles player Fred Hill, was diagnosed with leukemia at the age of three (3). In the second year of raising money for the Leukemia Society of America, the Eagles General Manager Jim Murray worked with local McDonald's franchise owners to have the team quarterback, Roman Gabriel, promote its shamrock shake in exchange for a share of the profits donated to the purchase of a house for young patients' families. The McDonald's owners came up with another idea. They offered to donate all the profits on the condition the house be named The Ronald McDonald House. There are now 302 Ronald McDonald Houses in 30 countries. Children's illness do affect people; who would have thought one little girl's leukemia would have made such a great difference!

Have you heard of Paul Butler? He was a student finishing his last year of school at North-East London Polytechnic in 1977. He was passionate about conservation and had spent several weeks finishing a field research project on the Caribbean island of St. Lucia. In particular he was concerned about the St. Lucia Parrot as there were only 110 left on the island. The population had been decimated due to their habitat being destroyed by developers as well as hunters and individuals who collected the parrots as pets. Upon graduation, Paul was offered a job by the St. Lucia Department of Forestry for six (6) months being paid $200 a month to implement his ideas and save the parrots! With little authority, time and money, Paul embarked on a campaign to change attitudes among the St. Lucian people about the parrot. He worked to help them embrace the parrot as part of their national identity. Support for the parrot rose, poaching stopped completely and there are now between 600 and 700 parrots on the island! One man with some ideas and little resources at his disposal was able to make a difference! What can you do to make a difference in a part of the world with the resources you have at your disposal?

_____

_____

_____

_____

Making a Difference®

What do WWE Champion, Hulk Hogan,

WWE Superstar John Cena NASCAR drivers Jeff Gordon and
Dale Earnhardt, Jr. have in common? All four (4) celebrities
have granted 200 wishes through the Make-A-Wish Foundation which helps children with life threatening medical
conditions. If these celebrities can find time in their busy
schedules to make a difference in the lives of children, what
can you do in your community to make a difference?

_____

_____

_____

_____

_____

_____

_____

_____

_____

_____

_____

_____

_____

_____

_____

Making a Difference®

Have you heard about the Lewis family? They are one family that has done twelve (12) good deeds on six (6) continents. It all began with a question in the fall of 2010. Jackson, who was 12 at the time, asked his dad, "Why aren't we doing more to make a difference?" His dad was taken aback and suggested initially that they volunteer locally. But then he said, "Let's do 12 in 12...12 projects, 12 countries, 12 months." And that is exactly what they did...from helping an orphanage in Beijing to an elementary school in Rawanda... they made a difference! Thank you to the Lewis family for sharing their example!

_____

_____

_____

_____

_____

_____

_____

_____

_____

_____

_____

_____

_____

_____

_____

Making a Difference®

A high school friend of mine shared with me how she makes a difference via mentoring. She works a few days a week at a psychiatric hospital for children. Recently, she was talking to a 14 year old girl who feels that she deserves to hurt herself. My former classmate says, "I know just my smile and a few minutes of my day makes all the difference in her world. It helps her to find the strength within her to help herself!" Kudos to my longtime friend for she is making a difference!

TIP OF THE DAY

Make A Difference Day is celebrated annually on the 4th Saturday in October. What will you be doing to participate? Make A Difference Day was started in 1990 by *USA Weekend* magazine. Its 20+ year history brings people together to tackle small and large needs in their communities. It's cited as America's largest day of doing good thanks to the commitment of millions of people willing to give of their time. What will you do on this weekend to make a difference?

Making a Difference®

Have you ever heard of the Elephant Nature Park in Chiang Mai, Thailand? It is an elephant rescue and rehabilitation center located in northern Thailand that LMDA Associate Kristen visited. It is also a place where you can volunteer. Check it out (elephantnaturepark.org) and see if you might be able to learn something new and make a difference!

Making a Difference®

Karen Duffy "Duff" Lambros

was the first VJ for MTV and is an amazing philanthropist always looking for ways to give back. She recently shared with me information about the Red Scarf Project which is dedicated to providing red scarves to children in foster care. Check it out and see how you might make a red scarf (yes there are directions on the website) as well as the timeframe to donate (September 1 – December 15th each year). See how making a red scarf can make a difference!

Making a Difference®

I attended the baby shower of my friend Cibeline. Instead of asking the guests to spend time watching her open the gifts, she asked each of us to spend time sharing a piece of advice with her about best parenting tips. Even though almost half of us in the room had never had children, we were each able to offer advice from how to use the rectal thermometer right away to remember to make time for yourself! It was a fun way to get to know the other attendees and exchange some ideas. And I know for sure we made a difference not only to Cibeline but to each other!

_____

_____

_____

_____

_____

_____

_____

_____

_____

_____

_____

_____

_____

_____

_____

Making a Difference®

In 2012 it was reported that an anonymous California donor gave a new animal rescue organization in Detroit a $1.5 million gift dedicated to building the city's first no-kill shelter. The Detroit Dog Rescue, founded by the TV producer Monica Martino and Hip-Hop artist Daniel (Hush) Carlisle, said they received the gift in stock options after a news report showcased their work in finding and rehabilitating the thousands of stray dogs in Detroit. Three (3) people and a news program doing something to make a difference!

Making a Difference®

Most of us have heard of Anne Frank, the young girl who is a symbol of courage during the Holocaust. Have you heard about Nadja Halilbegovich? She is known as the "Bosnian Anne Frank". As a young girl, Nadja survived the war in her native country of Bosnia and was injured by a bomb at age 13. By telling her story, she has brought her message of peace and hope to over 500,000 people throughout the world. One person telling her story of survival and making a difference!

Making a Difference ®

I recently saw a photo from the days when Adolph Hitler ruled Germany and was beginning to terrorize the world. The photo was taken in Hamburg in 1936, during the celebrations for the launch of the ship. In the crowd, one person refuses to raise his arm to give the Nazi salute. The man's name was August Landmesser. He had already been in trouble with the authorities, having been sentenced to two (2) years hard labor for simply marrying a Jewish woman. We know little about August Landmesser, except that he had two (2) children. By happenstance, chance or coincidence, one of his two children recognized her father in the photo when it was published in a German newspaper in 1991. While she must have been proud she must also have realized that one person, by simply refusing to raise his arm, truly did make a difference.

_____

_____

_____

_____

_____

_____

_____

_____

_____

_____

Johann Wolfgang von Goethe

said, "Whatever you do, or dream you can, begin it. Boldness has genius and power and magic in it." I would add that boldness also allows you to make a difference! Be bold today!

Making a Difference®

$\mathcal{D}r.\ \mathcal{J}ohn\ \mathcal{C}arlos$ is an Olympian, activist and author. During the 1968 Olympics he and Tommie Smith's Black Power salute on the Olympic podium produced controversy that affected his career. Yet that one simple act...standing with a fist raised in the air...is remembered and seen as an iconic image of Olympic history. John and Tommie definitely made a difference that year in 1968 that is still making a difference today!

_____

_____

_____

_____

_____

_____

_____

_____

_____

_____

_____

_____

_____

_____

_____

_____

_____

_____

Making a Difference®

Jennifer Pozner is the Executive Director of Women in the Media and News. She is also the author of *Reality Bites Back: the Troubling Truth About Guilty Pleasure TV* in which she reveals who is creating the pop culture backlash against women's rights and social progress as well as who is making a profit from it. Jennifer is making us take an in-depth look at how reality TV affects our beliefs, our culture and ultimately our behavior. She is definitely making a difference!

Making a Difference®

Have you heard about the nonprofit organization Create Jobs for USA? According to the literature, it's a project we can all be part of that can help our country recover. It is a project of Americans helping Americans to create, and most importantly, sustain jobs. Check it out (createjobsforUSA.org). See how Starbucks has become a partner and what change is happening. By simply going to the website and taking time to learn you will be making a difference!

_____

_____

_____

_____

_____

_____

_____

_____

_____

_____

_____

_____

_____

_____

_____

_____

Making a Difference®

$\mathcal{D}$id you know there is a Donor Bill of Rights? Yes, there are ten (10) rights you have as a donor that you should be aware of when considering making a donation. Check them out by going to charitynavigator.org. These are the nonprofit sector's industry standards and all charities should subscribe to them. Before you begin making a difference by providing a contribution, know your rights as a donor!

_____

_____

_____

_____

_____

_____

_____

_____

_____

_____

_____

_____

_____

_____

_____

_____

_____

_____

_____

_____

TIP OF THE DAY

When Autumn arrives, many of us get our home ready for the next season. Nonprofit organizations often do this, too, especially if they own their building. Call your favorite nonprofit to see what you can do to help them prepare for winter. You will be surprised how easy it is to make a difference!

Making a Difference®

TIP OF THE DAY

United Way campaigns take place in communities across the country. Remember the important work they do in your community and then consider participating in your company's workplace campaign via payroll deductions. Trust me, you won't miss those dollars and will definitely be making a difference!

_____

_____

_____

_____

_____

_____

_____

_____

_____

_____

_____

_____

_____

_____

_____

_____

_____

_____

Make the first day of Fall the time you begin thinking about what you want to do at the year-end in terms of your charitable donations. If you have a limited charitable budget, think about what is important to you and how you can provide charitable support. Easy ways to begin is giving up that daily cup of coffee, newspaper or evening out dining and use those savings as donations to your favorite causes! By doing this you will be making a difference!

TIP OF THE DAY

Are you looking for a job or a career change? Consider becoming an AmeriCorps VISTA (Volunteers in Service to America) participant. VISTA workers commit to working one year at a nonprofit or local government agency in many areas. Check it out (americorps.gov). You can make a difference!

Making a Difference ®

Are you trying to support a nonprofit organization but have a limited budget? Consider donating items that you normally purchase such as a book of stamps, a can of coffee, paper cups or reams of paper to your favorite charitable cause. When you buy one for yourself, buy one for your favorite charity. There are items that are always needed by nonprofit organizations. By doing something so simple, you can make a difference.

$\mathcal{D}o$ $\textit{you}$ $\textit{want}$ $\textit{to}$ volunteer but don't think you have the time? Consider "virtual volunteering" as an option. Almost anyone can do it i.e., older individuals, disabled individuals, stay at home moms, attorneys, marketing executives, etc.; you determine your volunteer hours and volunteer when it fits into your schedule. Call your favorite nonprofit organization and ask how you can be a volunteer virtually to make a difference!

Making a Difference®

We all need to work to make a difference in the lives of others. Start today by having a conversation with someone about your charitable efforts as well as learning more about theirs. Exchanging information with others will bring philanthropy to the forefront of people's attention and will start the ripple effect of making a difference!

Making a Difference®

September is Big Brothers Big Sisters Awareness Month. Have you thought about being a Big Brother or Big Sister? Do you know someone who would benefit from this type of program? If the answer to either one of these questions is yes, then go to bbbs.org and type in your zip code to find your local chapter information and see how easily you can begin making a difference.

TIP OF THE DAY

𝒱olunteer at your local school! August and September are back to school months in most communities! Find a way to begin making a difference in the lives of children through volunteering at their schools!

_____
_____
_____
_____
_____
_____
_____
_____
_____
_____
_____
_____
_____
_____
_____
_____
_____
_____
_____
_____
_____
_____
_____

Random acts of kindness do make a difference! With all the hustle and bustle in our lives, take time this day to do something nice for someone else. Hold a door open, offer to help someone who is struggling, be it with a life situation or simply putting a package in their car or cart, etc. Take a moment to make a difference...you will be joy-filled for rest of the day!

Making a Difference®

They say charity begins at home! Take some time today to make sure all those you care about are ok; make phone calls, send emails – communicate! Make sure your family and friends have all they need. Tell someone you care and see how it makes a difference.

Making a Difference®

Have you heard of Neighborhood Fruit (neighborhoodfruit.com)? It is an organization that was created due to the abundant fruit grown in backyards in urban areas, much of which goes to waste. The organization lists more than 10,000 registered fruit and nut trees nationally. By going to the website, individuals can locate trees that are close to them and pick the fruit for free. What an incredibly clever idea and a simple way to make a difference!

TIP OF THE DAY

Yesterday at lunch with friends, they told me about a new tradition started last year of giving their grandsons five $5 bills with instructions for them to donate it to someone or something. This year, the grandsons, ages six and nine, were already making plans for how to help others! What a difference you can make by teaching philanthropy to children!

Making a Difference®

Returning home, I saw billboards stating that kids by the age of twelve (12) have tried alcoholic beverages. Talk Sooner (Talksooner.org) is advocating that as early as ten (10) years old we begin talking to kids about alcohol. Check out the advice on the website and begin having conversations to make a difference!

_____

_____

_____

_____

_____

_____

_____

_____

_____

_____

_____

_____

_____

_____

_____

_____

_____

_____

Making a Difference®

Do you want to de-clutter your home but don't know where to begin? Think about Goodwill Industries. Most of us know the Goodwill stores in our communities to which we donate "used" goods, but did you know they also focus on job training and employment? In 2008, more than 1.5 million people were helped in this capacity. Think about getting involved with Goodwill by donating the items from your home as you de-clutter. You will be making a difference!

_____

_____

_____

_____

_____

_____

_____

_____

_____

_____

_____

_____

_____

_____

_____

_____

_____

Making a Difference®

Have you made your donations to charity this year? If not, there is still time. Remember your charitable donations must be postmarked by December 31st at 11:59 pm in order to be tax deductible this year. You can still make a difference!

_____

_____

_____

_____

_____

_____

_____

_____

_____

_____

_____

_____

_____

_____

_____

_____

_____

_____

_____

_____

Making a Difference®

What can you do to help those in poverty and struggling to make ends meet? What about providing new socks to the homeless? Socks are important to good health of homeless people and others - and they're often not donated. Donate new socks to your local homeless shelter or poverty-focused nonprofit. Socks and you can make a difference!

Making a Difference®

Statistics show that up to 47% of the adults in the City of Detroit are functionally illiterate. The issue of adult illiteracy is not just a Detroit problem. Across the U.S. many adults struggle with reading. An estimated 42 million Americans cannot read, write or even perform simple math. The number of functionally illiterate adults is estimated to increase by approximately 2.25 million people each year. Reading Works has a mission dedicated to raising the level of adult literacy in Metro Detroit and promoting the idea that Reading Works – in the family and in the workplace. Reading Works and it's literacy group partners are making a difference!

Making a Difference®

A quote I recently read said, "The most satisfying thing in life is to have been able to give a large part of one-self to others." That is what volunteering and being a donor does! Thanks to all who have made a donation, volunteered or somehow helped someone else! Your efforts do make a difference.

TIP OF THE DAY

When a loved one dies, most of us are sad and grieve, but often we forget that the young children in our families are grieving, too. The National Alliance for Grieving Children (grievingchildren.org) is a place to find resources and centers throughout the country. Check it out and use it as a resource to make a difference in the lives of children who've also suffered a loss!

Making a Difference®

I had the privilege of hearing former ABC Anchor Bob Woodruff speak about his traumatic brain injury. Injured in Iraq while reporting on the war, Bob made a miraculous recovery! His inspirational story continues through his Bob Woodruff Foundation. The Foundation supports ReMIND.org which works to heal the physical and psychological effects of war. Check it out and see how Bob and others are definitely making a difference!

When there is a cold freeze or freezing temperatures in your community, you might wonder what you can do to help and stay warm. A real easy action is to check on family members and neighbors. Make a phone call, offer to help someone who is struggling in the cold or simply start the car to warm it up for those in your family going somewhere! By pulling together and doing these relatively easy things to insure everyone in our community has heat and is safe, you will be making a difference!

TIP OF THE DAY

Did you know that more than three (3) million people in the United States live with epilepsy? The Epilepsy Foundation is a national nonprofit organization providing information and support to those living with this medical condition. Check out the website (epilepsyfoundation.org) to learn how you can make a difference to someone who has this condition!

By now you probably have heard that country crooner Glen Campbell has Alzheimer's. Every seventy (70) seconds, someone develops Alzheimer's with more than 5.3 million people having the disease in the United States. Did you know it is also the seventh (7th) leading cause of death? Check out more facts as well as the warning signs by visiting the Alzheimer's Association website (alz.org). There are ways you can get involved and make a difference to create a world without this terrible disease of Alzheimer's.

Making a Difference®

It has been more than ten (10) years since the 9/11 terrorist attacks on America. The United 93 Memorial located in Shanksville, Pennsylvania was dedicated in September 2011 but it still needs contributions to complete the fundraising efforts. Check it out (honorflight93.org) and consider making a donation. You will be honoring those courageous individuals on this flight who made a difference!

Making a Difference®

Did you know that 200,000 children are homeless every day? Did you know that more than 150,000 veterans are homeless at any given time! We can and must do better! Check out the facts and how you can help by going to the National Coalition for the Homeless (nationalhomeless. org). By working together, we can make a difference to end homelessness!

TIP OF THE DAY

Martin Luther King, Jr. said, "If a man
is called to be a street sweeper, he should sweep streets even as Michelangelo painted, or Beethoven composed music, or Shakespeare wrote poetry. He should sweep streets so well that all the hosts of heaven and earth will pause to say, here lived a great street sweeper who did his job well." Follow this advice. No matter what you do, do it well! You will be making a difference!

TIP OF THE DAY

Do you watch the Olympic Games? Did you know there's fundraising associated with all the US Olympic Teams? Yes, athletes and the various teams from the United States need to raise money to compete. They do this through corporate sponsorships and other fundraising means. Consider making a donation so these athletes can compete and continue to make a difference!

TIP OF THE DAY

Take care of your health! It is one of the most important things you can do! By leading a healthier lifestyle you set an example to young people in your life as well as insuring as you grow older you will remain healthy. Diabetes, heart disease, obesity, etc. are indicators of your health. Think about what you can do today to begin living and leading a healthy lifestyle. Work today to make a difference in your own life!

_____

_____

_____

_____

_____

_____

_____

_____

_____

_____

_____

_____

_____

_____

_____

_____

_____

_____

_____

Making a Difference®

TIP OF THE DAY

Childhood obesity is at epidemic rates with 25 million, or 32% of kids and adolescents, being overweight. First Lady Michelle Obama tackled this issue working with several US Departments and organizations to begin the Let's Move (letsmove.gov) campaign. Think about healthy food choices and what you can do to make a difference in this battle with childhood obesity!

Making a Difference®

TIP OF THE DAY

Volunteers give their time; donors give their money; board members give both. Are your nonprofit activities clearly identified and categorized? If not, give some thought to the appropriate role you can fill. You will make a difference by determining where you can best contribute your efforts.

A friend shared this story on Facebook and I love it because it shows how one person can make a difference. This is what he shared: "On Tuesday, I stopped at the Pontiac Speedway on my way to work at Oakland University. As I approached the door, there was a young boy standing there asking for gas money. I asked why he needed gas money. He said so his mother could drive him to school. Upon further questioning, he told me he was in second grade at Logan Elementary School located in Detroit, Michigan. I asked why he was so far from school and he replied that they had been at his mommy's boyfriend's house. He had about $2 in change. He shared that his mom said they needed at least $4 to get there. She was parked at pump number eight in a Chrysler 300. I told him I'd give him the difference so we went inside. While standing in line, I asked if he had eaten breakfast. Hearing him say no, I asked if he liked egg sandwiches. Seeing his smile, I grabbed an egg biscuit sandwich and handed it to him. I paid for my pop, his egg sandwich and put $4 on pump number 8. He said, "Thanks, mister" then went to pump the gas in the car. As I watched them drive away and get on I-75 I hoped I'd made a difference in that kid's life." I know my friend Mike did make a difference!

TIP OF THE DAY

Greg Anderson who is a best-selling author and founder of the American Wellness Project said, "When we are motivated by goals that have deep meaning, by dreams that need completion, by pure love that needs expressing, then we truly live life." I would add you are also well positioned to make a difference!

_____

_____

_____

_____

_____

_____

_____

_____

_____

_____

_____

_____

_____

_____

_____

_____

_____

_____

_____

_____

_____

_____

_____

Famed artist Andy Warhol said, "They always say time changes things, but you actually have to change them yourself." What do you see in your community that needs to be changed? As Andy Warhol says, you have to change them! Taking action will definitely make a difference!

TIP OF THE DAY

$\mathcal{F}$amed inventor Thomas Edison said, "I am not discouraged, because every wrong attempt discarded is another step forward." Don't give up! You could be one wrong attempt away from a step that truly makes a difference!

American social writer Eric Hoffer said, "Our greatest weariness comes from work not done." What is not done in your life or community? Think about it then do something. Action and work being done will definitely make a difference!

Making a Difference®

Swedish scientist Emanuel Swedenborg is quoted as saying, "Kindness is an inner desire that makes us want to do good things even if we do not get anything in return. It is the joy of our life to do them. When we do good things from this inner desire, there is kindness in everything we think, say and do." Powerful words to consider as you go through your day. Kindness definitely makes a difference!

Making a Difference®

Virgil, the great ancient Roman poet, is credited with writing, "They can because they think they can." Change your attitude. Take on that extra volunteer project. Make that additional donation to a nonprofit organization. Do what you can today because you think you can. It will make a difference!

_____

_____

_____

_____

_____

_____

_____

_____

_____

_____

_____

_____

_____

_____

_____

_____

_____

_____

_____

TIP OF THE DAY

American born minister and author Norman Vincent Peale is quoted as saying, "Practice hope. As hopefulness becomes a habit, you can achieve a permanently happy spirit." Try it and see how being hopeful and happy makes a difference!

Famed US General George S. Patton said, "Accept the challenges, so that you may feel the exhilaration of victory." What challenge is facing you and your community? Is there a river to be cleaned up? A library in need of books? A school program or project you could help? Follow General Patton's advice. Take up the challenge! You will be making a difference!

_____

_____

_____

_____

_____

_____

_____

_____

_____

_____

_____

_____

_____

_____

_____

_____

_____

_____

Koch Industries CEO Charles Koch said, "Our vision controls the way we think and, therefore, the way we act....the vision we have of our job determines what we do and the opportunities we see or don't see." What is your job? Do you see the opportunities? How can you make a difference by simply doing your job?

_____

_____

_____

_____

_____

_____

_____

_____

_____

_____

_____

_____

_____

_____

_____

_____

_____

_____

_____

Theodore "Teddy" Roosevelt, the 26th

President of the United States, said, "We cannot do great things unless we're willing to do the small things that make up the sum of greatness." It's similar to the riddle asking how do you eat an elephant. The answer is always one bite at a time. Do the small things. They will eventually lead you to the place of making a difference!

_____

_____

_____

_____

_____

_____

_____

_____

_____

_____

_____

_____

_____

_____

_____

_____

_____

_____

Making a Difference®

I love this quote by famed playwright George Bernard Shaw. He stated, "If you have an apple and I have an apple and we exchange these apples then you and I will still each have one apple. But if you have an idea and I have an idea and we exchange these ideas, then each of us will have two ideas." Amazing words to consider and live by and if you do, it will definitely make a difference!

TIP OF THE DAY

American author, pamphleteer and radical Thomas Paine stated, "We have it in our power to begin the world again." Consider this statement everyday then realize you can make a difference!

_____

_____

_____

_____

_____

_____

_____

_____

_____

_____

_____

_____

_____

_____

_____

_____

_____

_____

_____

_____

_____

_____

_____

Making a Difference®

Famed scientist Albert Einstein said, "The most important motive for work in school and life is pleasure in work, pleasure in its result, and the knowledge of the value of the results to the community." Take pleasure in the work you do today and the way it makes a difference in your world.

Making a Difference®

TIP OF THE DAY

Harry S. Truman was the 33rd President of the United States. He is quoted as saying, "It is amazing what you can accomplish if you do not care who gets the credit." Is this your attitude when working on something with others? Try it. See how not caring about who gets the credit allows you to make an even bigger difference!

Making a Difference®

Former US Congressman, US Senator and Vice President Dan Quayle said, "The question in life is not whether you get knocked down. You will. The question is, are you ready to get back up, are you willing to get back up and fight for what you believe in?" This is a true statement. Remember to get back up when you are knocked down. It is the getting back up that makes a difference!

Making a Difference®

Sydney J. Harris, a journalist for the *Chicago Daily News* and later the *Chicago Sun-Times*, said, "When I hear somebody sigh that "Life is hard," I am always tempted to ask, "Compared to what?" Use this advice. Don't let the fact that something might be hard deter you from working to making a difference.

The 32nd President of the United States Franklin Delano Roosevelt said, "There is a mysterious cycle in human events. To some generations much is given. Of other generations much is expected. This generation of Americans has a rendezvous with destiny." He was speaking of the men and women who would have to sacrifice much during World War II. Reporter and author Tom Brokaw has called that group of men and women the 'greatest generation', writing books detailing their efforts. What is your generation's destiny? What are you doing to meet the challenges and make a difference?

_____

_____

_____

_____

_____

_____

_____

_____

_____

_____

_____

_____

_____

_____

Making a Difference®

American Olympian and gold medalist Geoffrey Gaberino said, "The real contest is always between what you've done and what you're capable of doing. You measure yourself against yourself and nobody else." I love this statement. What are you capable of doing to make a difference in your world?

_____

_____

_____

_____

_____

_____

_____

_____

_____

_____

_____

_____

_____

_____

_____

_____

_____

_____

_____

TIP OF THE DAY

French poet, essayist and philosopher Paul Valery said, "The best way to make your dreams come true is to wake up." Wake up. Work today for your dreams in order to make a difference in your world.

Making a Difference®

American minister and philanthropist Russell H. Conwell said, "Your diamonds are not in far distant mountains or in yonder seas; they are in your own backyard, if you but dig for them." Sometimes we think it would be easier to change something or make a difference if we lived somewhere else, had a different job, or were born into a different life. None of these matter; look in your own backyard to find your treasure and continue making a difference!

Famed entrepreneur Walt Disney said, "When you believe in a thing, believe in it all the way, implicitly and unquestionable." What could you believe in today that your belief will make the difference?

_____

_____

_____

_____

_____

_____

_____

_____

_____

_____

_____

_____

_____

_____

_____

_____

_____

_____

_____

_____

_____

_____

Making a Difference®

What do Hillary Clinton, Reese Witherspoon, Laura Bush, Dakota Fanning, Katie Couric and many other women have in common? They were all Girl Scouts during their youth. In 2012, the Girl Scouts celebrated their 100 year anniversary. Founded in Savannah, Georgia by Juliette Gordon Low, the first troop was comprised of 18 girls. Now more than 3.2 million girls are Girl Scouts. One woman with a vision changing so many lives! Juliette Gordon Low definitely made a difference!

Making a Difference®

In 2012, singer and songwriter Kellie Pickler shared that she will donate all the proceeds from her part in the Dodge Ram Truck "Road to the Ram Jam" concert that took place in Nashville to the USO. She stated, "I've loved taking a little piece of home to our troops in Iraq and Afghanistan." Kellie Pickler is definitely making a difference!

Making a Difference®

One of my favorite songs is "Angels Among Us" by the group Alabama. The refrain lines of the song are, "Oh I believe there are angels among us. Sent down to us from somewhere up above. They come to you and me in our darkest hours. To show us how to live, to teach us how to give. To guide us with a light of love." Who are the angels in your life? Have you told them how much they mean to you? Tell them they make a difference in your life.

_____

_____

_____

_____

_____

_____

_____

_____

_____

_____

_____

_____

_____

_____

_____

Making a Difference®

Founding Father Benjamin Franklin said, "Tell me and I forget. Teach me and I remember. Involve me and I learn." Powerful words to live by and by doing so you will definitely make a difference!

_____
_____
_____
_____
_____
_____
_____
_____
_____
_____
_____
_____
_____
_____
_____
_____
_____
_____
_____
_____
_____
_____

TIP OF THE DAY

I love the writings of Anais Nin. She said, "And the day came when the risk to remain tight in the bud was more painful than the risk it took to blossom." What has been bothering you that you think you can't do anything about? Risk it today and see what happens. By simply being willing to change you will be making a difference!

_____

_____

_____

_____

_____

_____

_____

_____

_____

_____

_____

_____

_____

_____

_____

_____

_____

_____

_____

_____

My friend, Nadine, shared the following,

"Bread cast on the water comes back to you. The good deed you do today may benefit you or someone you love at the least expected time. If you never see the deed again at least you will have made the world a better place....after all, isn't that what life is all about?" And isn't this the way to make a difference?

Making a Difference®

Famed poet and author W.H. Auden once wrote, "Let all your thinks be thanks." Take some time to connect with the people and organizations you think about to give them your thanks for being in your life and community. Think about the difference you could make with your show of appreciation!

_____

_____

_____

_____

_____

_____

_____

_____

_____

_____

_____

_____

_____

_____

_____

_____

_____

_____

Making a Difference®

It is said famed inventor Thomas Edison conducted over 9,000 experiments before figuring out the best way to make a light bulb. What are you struggling to do that will change your world? Don't give up. By being persistent you can make a difference!

Making a Difference®

Try this exercise: can you think of 100 ways you could make a difference in your life and the lives of others? Start this exercise today and see how simply thinking about ways to make a difference really does cause a difference to be made.

_____

_____

_____

_____

_____

_____

_____

_____

_____

_____

_____

_____

_____

_____

_____

_____

_____

_____

_____

_____

_____

_____

Making a Difference®

There is a Chinese proverb that states, "The temptation to quit is greatest just before you are about to succeed." Don't give up. The ability to succeed and make a difference is just around the corner and might just happen tomorrow.

Making a Difference ®

My friend Monica always sends information about voting for judges just before each election, both the primary and the general. This simple act of helping inform her friends about the resources and choices available really does make a difference!

Making a Difference®

Holly Petraeus, wife of General David Petraeus, is a compassionate and caring person. During her husband's tenure in the military she would meet soldiers returning home, especially those who did not have family members greetings them when they returned from a tour of duty. This simple act by Holly Petraeus made a difference!

Making a Difference®

Veterans Day is a day of reflection. Take time on this year's day of recognition to thank a veteran for what they did. With so many veterans returning from the current war, there are things you can do to help. For example, consider hiring a vet for open positions in your company; make a donation to one of the many veteran/military nonprofits such as the Wounded Warrior Project or the USO; visit a VA Hospital and provide some cheer and comfort or offer up a prayer of thanks. These are only some of things you could do that would make a difference. What will you do to make a difference today?

My friend, Lori, shared the following on one of her Facebook posts, "What creative ways can I contribute with ease, joy, and glory today?" What creative ways can you use to make a difference?

_____

_____

_____

_____

_____

_____

_____

_____

_____

_____

_____

_____

_____

_____

_____

_____

_____

_____

_____

_____

Making a Difference®

It seems like a simple thing to do but I take the time to cut the box tops from my various grocery and food items. I save these for the school of the children, Joseph and Jack, who live next door. When I have collected a few, I drop them off in an envelope in their mailbox. I find this a really easy way to make a difference!

Making a Difference®

In 2011, President Obama, Vice President Biden, First Lady Obama and Dr. Jill Biden launched *Joining Forces*. This is a national initiative to honor and support America's service members and their families. The purpose is to educate, challenge, and spark action from all sectors of our society including citizens, communities, businesses, nonprofit organizations, faith based institutions, philanthropic organizations, and government. Check it out (joiningforces.gov) and see how you could get involved to help to make a difference!

Making a Difference®

An acquaintance named Lane traveled to Nicaragua with 4 other friends and his son. They were on a mission to help local people. They discovered much and learned how blessed they are to be living in the USA. But in addition to their learning, they decided to do something. They came back to the United States determined to raise funds to feed the children and help some who were living in the dump to be placed in a home. Because of their efforts, everyday 110 children are fed. But Lane does something else. He sets his watch to beep at noon; when it does, it causes him to pause and remember that because of him and his friends' efforts, children are eating. Lane and his friends are definitely making a difference!

Making a Difference®

Actor Matt Damon said, "I tell [my kids] it's important to be involved in the world in the ways that help others and not just yourself." Thanks Matt for sharing very good advice with your children and now us! You are making a difference!

Winston Churchill, Great Britain's Prime

Minister during World War II, said, "Perhaps it is better to be irresponsible and right then to be responsible and wrong." Sometimes you have to just go for it when you know it will make a difference!

My friend Aimee gave me a card that had a depiction of an older woman carrying a closed umbrella and jumping off the curb into the muddied street in white strap sandals. The caption on the card, from an unknown Hollywood script writer, says, "Ever notice that "what the hell" is always the right decision?" So true and by following this advice, you will surely make a difference!

Making a Difference®

My friend Tara gave me a book titled, *The Paper Bag Princess*. It's a different take on the much read tales of ladies waiting for their princes to come and rescue them. It is written in the format of a child's story but has a powerful message for all of us. Check it out! Thanks, Tara, for sharing this book and making a difference in my life!

Making a Difference®

Famed leader of the Latter Day Saints movement as well as a pioneer in the western US Brigham Young said, "True independence and freedom can only exist in doing what's right." Be independent and free today by doing what you know is right! You will be making a difference!

_____

_____

_____

_____

_____

_____

_____

_____

_____

_____

_____

_____

_____

_____

_____

_____

_____

_____

_____

_____

American author Mark Twain said, "When in doubt, tell the truth." Tell the truth about what you see and what you want to change. It will always make a difference!

$\mathcal{B}$usiness leader Peter F. Drucker said, "Effective leadership is not about making speeches or being liked; leadership is defined by results not attributes." I find this statement very true. Look for results when seeking out leaders. Leaders get results and thus are always able to make a difference!

_____

_____

_____

_____

_____

_____

_____

_____

_____

_____

_____

_____

_____

_____

_____

_____

_____

_____

_____

_____

_____

Making a Difference®

Many of us have heard this quote but I never knew former US President Dwight D. Eisenhower said it, "What counts is not necessarily the size of the dog in the fight, it's the size of the fight in the dog." Don't worry about what you don't have to change the world; focus on what you want to change, then go for it. You will be making a difference!

Roman poet and philosopher Lucretius said, "Constant dripping hollows out a stone." Keep working at what you want to change. Your constant effort will make a difference!

Making a Difference®

The 32nd US President Franklin D. Roosevelt said, "The only limit of our realization of tomorrow will be our doubts of today. Let us move forward with strong and active faith." Follow this advice. Eliminate your doubts and you will be sure to change the world and make a difference!

Making a Difference®

TIP OF THE DAY

I love this quote by American author Napoleon Hill. He said, "Do not wait; the time will never be just right." Follow this advice. What are you thinking about doing today that will change your community or an individual's world? Tackle it today and you will be assured you will be making a difference!

_____

Making a Difference®

Many of us can instantly recall the name of the company associated with the tagline "Just do it." The company is Nike. While the phrase is simple, it is memorable. What simple thing could you do today that will be memorable and make a difference?

_____

_____

_____

_____

_____

_____

_____

_____

_____

_____

_____

_____

_____

_____

_____

_____

_____

_____

_____

_____

_____

Making a Difference®

American novelist, essayist, playwright, poet and social critic James Arthur Baldwin said, "Not everything that is faced can be changed. But nothing can be changed until it is faced." Powerful and true words to live your life by and in doing so you will definitely be making a difference!

My friend Sandra began her philanthropic involvement journey by gathering some friends together to feed those less fortunate in her community in New Mexico! Now she actively looks for people in her community that need help. Once she determines what she wants to do, she enlists her family and friends to help. Sandra is one person really looking in her community for ways she can make a difference!

_____

_____

_____

_____

_____

_____

_____

_____

_____

_____

_____

_____

_____

_____

_____

_____

_____

_____

Making a Difference®

American author and minister Norman Vincent Peale said, "Never talk defeat. Use words like hope, belief, faith, victory." Try to use only positive words for just today. See how it changes your outlook and makes a difference in your attitude.

_____

_____

_____

_____

_____

_____

_____

_____

_____

_____

_____

_____

_____

_____

_____

_____

_____

_____

_____

_____

_____

Making a Difference®

Pittsburgh Pirates baseball player Jerry Lynch said, "When you believe and think "I can," you activate your motivation, commitment, confidence, concentration and excitement – all of which relate directly to achievement." Change your thinking to "I can" in whatever you are attempting to do or change in your world. I believe it will definitely make a difference!

Making a Difference ®

One of the Founding Fathers, Benjamin Franklin, said, "He that can have patience can have what he will." Change sometimes comes slowly. Don't give up. By simply having patience you will be making a difference!

_____

_____

_____

_____

_____

_____

_____

_____

_____

_____

_____

_____

_____

_____

_____

_____

_____

_____

_____

_____

Famed cowboy Will Rogers said, "We can't all be heroes because somebody has to sit on the curb and clap as they go by." I love this quote because it illustrates that everyone has a role – whether hero or the "clapper". Each has a role to play and each makes a difference.

Making a Difference®

I receive a lot of appeals for financial support in the mail from nonprofit organizations. Most do not stand out, but one did. It was from the USO. It said, "The loneliest time...the holidays. Even a letter from home – though much desired – can bring up the pangs of loneliness." It asked me to help the USO bring a little holiday cheer to the more than 120,000 men and women in our military who can't get home for the holidays. The USO does amazing work. Consider making donation (uso.org) to this or one of the other nonprofits working to help our military personnel all year. You will be making a difference!

Making a Difference®

Albert Einstein once said, "You have to learn the rules of the game, and then play better than anyone else." What is something you don't know much about but want to change? Learn the game so that you can play better than anyone else and make a difference!

_____
_____
_____
_____
_____
_____
_____
_____
_____
_____
_____
_____
_____
_____
_____
_____
_____
_____
_____
_____
_____

TIP OF THE DAY

I love this quote by Winston Churchill, famed former Prime Minister of Great Britain, "Courage is what it takes to stand up and speak; courage is also what it takes to sit down and listen." What type of courage do you have? It will make a difference!

_____

_____

_____

_____

_____

_____

_____

_____

_____

_____

_____

_____

_____

_____

_____

_____

_____

_____

_____

_____

Sometimes we forget that small changes in our behavior can have a big impact. Leaving your car at home twice a week can help cut greenhouse gas emissions by 1,600 pounds per year! Instead, use public transportation, carpool, bike or walk to reduce air pollutants and make a green difference!

_____

_____

_____

_____

_____

_____

_____

_____

_____

_____

_____

_____

_____

_____

_____

_____

_____

_____

_____

Have you ever heard of Gaylord Nelson? He was a U.S. Senator of Wisconsin that was disturbed and frustrated by seeing the ravages of a 1969 Santa Barbara, California oil spill. In an effort to raise environmental consciousness, he advocated for the first Earth Day in April of 1970 which mobilized over 20 million Americans to rally in support of environmental reform, and now Earth Day is embraced over 180 participating countries. What is something you see that bothers you in your environment? Like Senator Nelson, you could have an idea that could make a difference worldwide!

_____

_____

_____

_____

_____

_____

_____

_____

_____

_____

_____

_____

_____

_____

Making a Difference®

Did you know that of all the water in the world, only 1% of it is suitable for human consumption? Water is a finite source that many organizations are trying to conserve. You can do your own part by doing some simple changes. Running your dishwasher only when it is full and not pre-washing dishes can save up to 20 gallons per load. Taking a 5-10 min shower instead of a bath can save over 50 gallons of water! Turning off the faucet when brushing your teeth will save unlimited gallons of water. Can you think of other ways to conserve and make a difference?

_____

_____

_____

_____

_____

_____

_____

_____

_____

_____

_____

_____

_____

Making a Difference®

TIP OF THE DAY

Making a list and checking it twice...most of us know this usually refers to Santa. However, have you made your list of charities you plan to support this year? Be sure to support your favorite causes now; don't let your charitable intent get lost in the hustle and bustle of the holidays! You can make a difference!

Making a Difference®

UNICEF is an organization that provides humanitarian relief to children all over the globe. But did you know that they sell handmade crafts from many different countries in support of UNICEF? Going to their website (UnicefUSA.org/shop) and shopping for cards and gifts will help save children's lives. You will be making a difference!

AARP's Drive to End Hunger

has paired with the Stamp Out Hunger Food Drive to allow you to make a difference by donating non-perishable food items from the comfort of your own mailbox. The National Associations of Letter Carriers in sponsorship with United States Postal Service, Feeding America, United Way, and many others promote awareness of hunger collection day where you can leave a bag of non-perishable food by your mailbox to be picked up by your letter carrier. Go to (help-stampouthunger.com) to learn more. Listen to their call to action: "Fill a bag with food. Bring hope to someone in need" and help make a difference!

Making a Difference®

Humanitarian and Former Major League Baseball shortstop and National Baseball Hall of Fame member, Cal Ripken, Jr., once said, "They said we'll never get this game going if you don't run around the field, I said I didn't have the energy to make it. They said, 'Then walk.'" He recently began working with Energizer and Habitat for Humanity to help the communities devastated by the May 2011 tornadoes in Joplin, Missouri. He reminds us that helping out and giving back doesn't need a lot of fanfare and excitement. It all begins with a first step and we can walk if we must. Thanks to Cal Ripken, Jr. for showing us how to access the All Star in all of us and for truly making a difference!

Making a Difference®

Have you ever heard of the Posse Foundation, Inc. (possefoundation.org)? Posse is a support program for multicultural youth that provides prep-collegiate training to a peer group or "posse" with the goal of having that group graduate from a 4-year college with a leadership network built on success. Thanks to the Posse Foundation for creating a unique organization that works in a multicultural world. You are making a difference.

Making a Difference®

Reading to young children helps foster close relationships and can be a fun family activity. Poet W.H. Auden once wrote, "There are good books which are only for adults. There are no good books which are only for children." Read with the children in your life and let a good book impact both you and the child. You will be making a difference!

Making a Difference®

Marcel Proust once wrote, "The real voyage of discovery consists not in seeking new landscapes but in having new eyes." What around you could you look at with new eyes? What will you discover? Doing this will show you new ways to go out and make a difference!

_____

_____

_____

_____

_____

_____

_____

_____

_____

_____

_____

_____

_____

_____

_____

_____

_____

_____

_____

_____

_____

Making a Difference®

Did you know that a donation of one pint of blood can save up to three lives? Go to americasblood. org or redcross.org/donate/give to learn more and to find donation centers. Make a difference in your community by learning how to host a blood drive or donating and you can help save lives!

Making a Difference®

Have you ever heard of Lyle and Sandy Reed? They are an Arizona couple who have fostered 160 kids in 28 years! They have adopted nine (9) of those foster children. Thanks to Lyle and Sandy Reed, who saw a need in their community and were able to open their hearts and their home. Think about how you can foster a need in your community to make a difference.

Making a Difference®

A friend of mine sent me a quote by American author, historian and clergyman, Edward Everett Hale that really got me thinking. It states, "I am only one, But still I am one. I cannot do everything, But still I can do something; And because I cannot do everything, I will not refuse to do the something that I can do. I am only one person but I can always do something." Use this profound statement to reflect on the good that you can do. It only takes one person to make a difference!

_____

_____

_____

_____

_____

_____

_____

_____

_____

_____

_____

_____

_____

_____

_____

_____

_____

Making a Difference®

Did you ever think that writing a letter to Santa helps make wishes come true? Annually, during the holiday season, Macy's collects letters addressed to Santa at The North Pole. Macy's counts them and for each letter they donate $1 to the Make-A-Wish Foundation up to $1 million for the year 2011. Check it out (macys.com/believe) and see how the very traditional act of writing a letter to Santa really does make a difference!

Never be afraid to seek inspiration even in odd places. A friend of mine sent me a silly little quote from Dr. Seuss. It states, "I have heard there are troubles of more than one kind. Some come from ahead and some come from behind. But I've bought a big bat. I'm all ready you see. Now my troubles are going to have troubles with me!" Facing the troubles around you and in your community with a plan of action will leave you prepared to hit them head on in order to make a difference!

_____

_____

_____

_____

_____

_____

_____

_____

_____

_____

_____

_____

_____

_____

_____

_____

_____

Making a Difference®

What do Courvoisier, Cruzan and Jim Beam have in common? They are familiar names in premium spirits and also brands of Beam, Inc., a company that has made a true commitment to social responsibility. They are currently partnered with Operation Homefront (operation-homefront.net), an organization that provides assistance for our troops, their families and wounded soldiers. Since 2008, Beam, Inc. has donated close to $2.5 million and many volunteer hours to the cause. Thanks to Beam, Inc. for making a difference!

Making a Difference®

J.K. Rowling, best-selling author of the Harry Potter series, once said, "We do not need magic to transform our world. We carry all of the power we need inside ourselves already." Use the power inside of you to transform your world. It doesn't take magic to live a charmed existence and make a difference

Making a Difference®

More than 300 million adults and children in the world suffer from poor vision because they cannot receive vision care or cannot afford glasses and eye exams. OneSight, a Luxottica Foundation (onesight.org), is seeking to provide healthy visions for people all over the world. You can do your part by donating your old, gently-used prescription eyeglasses to a LensCrafters store. You would be making a clear difference in someone's life!

Making a Difference®

Nonfunctioning and outdated electronics are quickly becoming a large portion of our waste stream. Americans discard an estimated 400 million pieces of these electronics or "e-waste" each year. These machines have toxic materials, such as lead, mercury, and brominated flame-retardants. The U.S. EPA estimates that over 80% of our e-waste ends up thrown away in American landfills and incinerators, contaminating our air, water and land. There is something you can do to makes sure that your e-waste does not end up in a landfill. Many manufacturers are now participants in take-back programs, where you can drop-off or mail-in your e-wastes and these companies have an obligation to make sure that these items are recycled responsibly. Check out sites like (www.productstewardship. net/productsElectronicsBizProgramsTakeback.html) to learn which manufacturers have responsible take-back programs. Getting in the habit of recycling electronics is a difference you can make for generations to come.

TIP OF THE DAY

William B. Sprague, an American clergymen, once said, "Do not wait to strike till the iron is hot; but make it hot by striking." What can you take initiative on today? Being preemptive and proactive in your approach to life will allow you to make new opportunities for yourself and make a difference in the world around you.

Making a Difference®

One of my friends recently sent me this bit of wisdom that she had forwarded to her soon-to-be a college graduate daughter. "Knowing is not enough; we must apply. Willing is not enough; we must do." This quote by Johann Wolfgang von Goethe lets us know that there is a time for learning, but beyond that, we must apply what we have learned to our lives. What do you know about in your community that you can apply yourself to change? What can you do to make a difference?

_____

_____

_____

_____

_____

_____

_____

_____

_____

_____

_____

_____

_____

_____

_____

_____

_____

Making a Difference®

Do you want to help those who have difficulty during the holiday season? Call your local Salvation Army office to find out what is still needed....remember, there is still time to make a difference!

Making a Difference®

Sometimes we can get wrapped up in our own little worlds and forget that we are all a part of the same human race. The famed poet W.B. Yeats said, "There are no strangers, only friends you have not met yet." Try talking to someone new as you go about your day. Who knows? You might be making a difference and making a new friend!

Making a Difference®

Tom's of Maine is a company doing great work. They are a manufacturer of all natural personal care products and great believer in the power of giving back. Annually they host their "50 States For Good" program, where they will award $150,000 to nonprofit groups for funding community projects. Go to the website (tomsofmaine.com) to learn more and apply! Thanks Tom's of Maine for making a difference!

Making a Difference®

ALS, also known as Lou Gehrig's disease, is a debilitating disease that affects the motor neurons in the brain and causes most people that develop the condition to die within three years. The ALS Association has made its mission to, "fight to treat and cure ALS through global research and nationwide advocacy while also empowering people with Lou Gehrig's disease and their families to live fuller lives by providing them with compassionate care and support." Go to their website (ALS.org) to learn how you can support the Association through the Walk to Defeat ALS or through donation. Thanks to the ALS Association for making a difference in the lives of the affected and in the fight for a cure.

Willow House is a nonprofit organization that helps families deal with the loss of loved ones. It is a member agency of the National Alliance for Grieving Children and helps provide resources to help children deal with grief. Thank you Willow House (willowhouse.org) for making a difference.

Making a Difference®

Have you heard of the Association of Donor Relations Professionals? The Association of Donor Relations Professionals (ADRP) is a nonprofit business league organized to encourage the professional development stewardship and the development of community. They help support the people who support donor relations. Thanks to this group for working to make a difference!

TIP OF THE DAY

$\mathcal{F}$amed author, speaker and holocaust survivor Elie Wiesel once said, "The opposite of love is not hate, it's indifference. The opposite of art is not ugliness, it's indifference. The opposite of faith is not heresy, it's indifference. And the opposite of life is not death, it's indifference." Love one another, have faith and live life without indifference. This will make a difference in your life.

Making a Difference®

Named in honor of Gloria Steinem, the Ms. Foundation's annual Gloria Awards is a salute to women of vision which honors the achievements of women activists and the supporters whose courage and leadership ignite change on behalf of women, families and communities. The Ms. Foundation Gloria Awards recognizes remarkable women and organizations making a difference!

Rabbi Harold Kushner is credited with saying, "If you concentrate on finding whatever is good in every situation, you will discover that your life will suddenly be filled with gratitude, a feeling that nurtures the soul." Think about the nonprofit organizations in your community doing amazing work. Be grateful for the work they are doing; take time to send a note or email telling them. This simple act of gratitude will make a difference!

Remember this bit of wisdom from Dr. Seuss, "Today you are You, that is truer than true. There is no one alive who is Youer than You." Making a difference starts with YOU!

Made in the USA
Charleston, SC
07 May 2013